Key Methods in Second Language Acquisition Research

Key Methods in Second Language Acquisition Research

Alessandro G. Benati

SHEFFIELD UK BRISTOL CT

Published by Equinox Publishing Ltd.

UK: Office 415, The Workstation, 15 Paternoster Row, Sheffield, South Yorkshire S1 2BX
USA: ISD, 70 Enterprise Drive, Bristol, CT 06010

www.equinoxpub.com

First published 2015

British Library Cataloguing-in-Publication Data

A catalogue record for this book is available from the British Library.

ISBN-13 978 1 78179 240 7 (hardback)
978 1 78179 241 4 (paperback)

Library of Congress Cataloging-in-Publication Data

Benati, Alessandro G., author.
Key methods in second language acquisition research / Alessandro G. Benati.
pages cm
Includes bibliographical references and index.
ISBN 978-1-78179-240-7 (hb) — ISBN 978-1-78179-241-4 (pb) 1. Second language acquisition—Research. 2. Language and languages—Study and teaching—Research. 3. Language teachers—Training of—Research. I. Title.
P118.2.B455 2015
401′.93—dc23
2015010609

Typeset by Apex CoVantage, LLC

Printed and bound in Great Britain by Lightning Source UK Ltd, Milton Keynes and Lightning Source Inc., La Vergne, TN

The book is dedicated to my father Orazio Filippo Benati

"Se si insegnasse la bellezza alla gente, la si fornirebbe di un'arma contro la rassegnazione, la paura e l'omertà. All'esistenza di orrendi palazzi sorti all'improvviso, con tutto il loro squallore, da operazioni speculative, ci si abitua con pronta facilità, si mettono le tendine alle finestre, le piante sul davanzale, e presto ci si dimentica di come erano quei luoghi prima, ed ogni cosa, per il solo fatto che è così, pare dover essere così da sempre e per sempre. È per questo che bisognerebbe educare la gente alla bellezza: perché in uomini e donne non si insinui più l'abitudine e la rassegnazione ma rimangano sempre vivi la curiosità e lo stupore (Peppino Impastato)"

Contents

Acknowledgements

I would like to thank my undergraduate, postgraduate and research students for giving me the opportunity and inspiration to write this book. The structure, the ideas and the way the book has been conceived is the fruit of both my interaction with research and the insightful discussions with all my students and colleagues.

A special thank you to Janet Joyce and Valerie Hall for accepting my proposal and working with me in the production of this manuscript.

A note of gratitude to Tanja Angelovska and the anonymous readers and colleagues for their constructive advice and valuable suggestions aimed at improving the content of this book.

Preface

This book is a basic manual written in an attempt to help novice teachers and undergraduate students to develop an awareness and understanding of the key methodological frameworks and processes used in second language research. The book should also help readers to generate ideas and researchable questions, to conduct research adopting a particular research framework and to develop a plan to collect and analyze data.

The aim of the book is fivefold: to develop the reader's skills in understanding, interpreting and analyzing basic components in second language research design; to develop the reader's ability to read second language research and to understand basic concepts and procedures; to develop the reader's awareness of the process and practicalities of conducting second language research; to provide the reader with the underpinning and basic knowledge to enable them to develop ideas; and to explore possible areas of research and research designs within a specific research methodological framework.

The book provides readers, in a very accessible way, with the basic tools to read, understand and conduct second language research (use of questionnaires, tests, observation schemes, surveys, psycholinguistic methods, etc.). Practical examples of studies conducted within each of the research frameworks presented in the book are provided.

The book is divided into three main parts: Key Stages in Second Language Research (Part One); Key Methodological Frameworks (Part Two); and Mixed Frameworks and Psycholinguistic Methods (Part Three).

Part One provides a generic introduction to second language research. The main goal of this first part of the book is to sketch the basics concepts for the novice reader and to identify the key components and key steps in second language research.

Part Two is written to introduce the novice reader to the basic concepts and components of each of the main research frameworks in second language research.

Each chapter makes use of exemplary studies to illustrate the key phases of various designs grouped into four main methodological frameworks (action research, experimental, observation, case study). To accomplish this, each chapter will contain the following features:

Key Concepts and Components
Key Data Collection and Analysis Procedures

Key Advantages and Disadvantages
Key Exemplary Study
Key Terms
Key Readings

In Part Three of this book mixed frameworks and psycholinguistic methods used in second language acquisition research will be described. In the concluding chapter, a brief summary of the main research components in second language research will be provided.

Chapter previews, examples, questions, tasks, references and suggestions for further reading are an integral part of each chapter in the book.

Part One

Key Stages in Second Language Research

This section of the book provides a generic introduction to second language research. The main goal of this first section is to sketch the basic concepts for the novice reader/researcher and to identify the key components (Chapter 1) and the key steps necessary to embark in second language research. Two exemplary studies, from two different methodological frameworks, will be used to illustrate how second language research is reported (Chapter 2).

1 What Are the Key Components in Second Language Research?

Chapter Preview

In this chapter a clear definition of second language research is provided. Similarities and differences between research as a natural process and research as a scientific method of enquiry will be presented. Research is a cyclical process which involves a number of interrelated phases such as producing literature reviews, formulating research questions and/or hypotheses, and developing a careful methodological plan to collect and analyze data. These phases will be analyzed and discussed. Key methodological frameworks will be briefly introduced. Qualitative and quantitative research will be defined. Ethical considerations in conducting second language research will also be considered.

1.1 What Is the Nature of Second Language Research?

Undergraduate and graduate students, practitioners and teachers who are about to embark on a second language research project should keep in mind the following points:

1. Always choose a topic that interests and fascinates you. The Latin root of the word 'study' is *studio* and means passion.
2. Always select a topic that is manageable within the time constraint. Feasibility is a key component in second language research.
3. Always keep in mind that simplicity is a virtue, particularly in research. The most successful and effective piece of research is one that has very clear objectives.
4. Always persevere and never give up. Frustration is the force behind much good and innovative research, and perseverance is one of the major ingredients in constructive research.

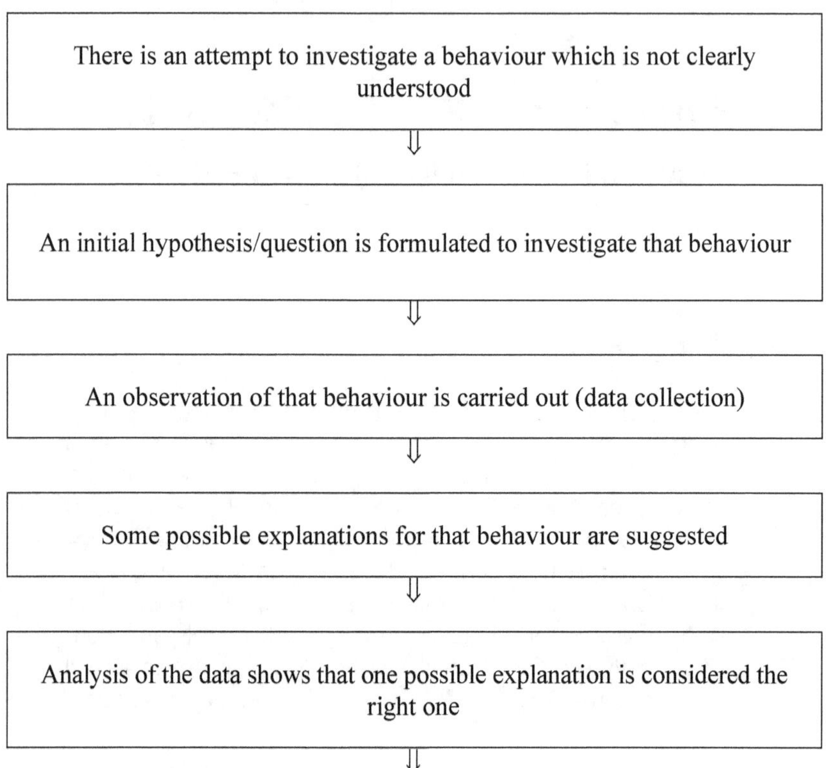

Figure 1.1 Definition of second language research

Having established what individual attributes a project should require, and what a researcher should keep in mind to be successful, the question to be addressed in this section is: What is second language research?

A minimal definition of second language research is that it involves a number of interlinked stages (see flowchart in Figure 1.1).

From an initial analysis, the above stages are not so different to what one sometimes does in the real world. In everyday life people observe phenomena which they cannot understand and they look for different ways to explain them. Teachers reflect on the behaviour of language learners and formulate hypotheses which they try to address through various actions in the attempt to resolve a particular problem. The key question here is: What is the difference between research as a natural process and research as a scientific process?

Research as a natural process is something we all do in everyday life. We often observe phenomena in the environment and we make a hypothesis about the relationships between a numbers of factors. We then take some actions to establish whether our hypothesis can be proved. Language teachers might come to the realization that a particular set of material is not effective in stimulating motivation among students. They might develop a new set of material and use it in the classroom. Later they might observe that students seem to be more engaged and therefore conclude that the 'new material' is the causative factor for students' improved motivation. The 'problem' with this more natural and direct approach to research is that it is not methodologically sound. Investigating the possible relationships between 'effective teaching materials' and an increase in students' motivation and performance would need to be approached in a more systematic, scientific and methodical way to be able to draw objective conclusions.

The difference between 'natural research' and 'scientific research' is that second language research must be systematic and methodical in order to provide objective, concrete and insightful information on how language acquisition happens, for instance, or what would be the best approach/technique for teaching languages. Although natural observations of phenomena are vital for making research advances in any field of enquiry, second language research must be conducted in a very methodical and scientific way to have a direct impact on the field of second language acquisition. The main aim of any research project is to obtain results which would provide scientific evidence to support or reject specific research questions or hypotheses and/or generate further ones. The results must be objectively valid and obtained through the use of scientific research methods. The research process must involve different stages, which need to be followed methodically. Often second language research involves gathering information, classification, analysis and interpretation of data to see to what extent the initial objectives have been achieved.

Second language research often has a theoretical scope. Researchers are interested in testing and verifying a theory to develop a better understanding of how learners comprehend, process and produce a second language. Researchers tend to address theoretical questions aimed at describing how learners develop an internal system and eventually are able to tap into that system for speech production. However, despite the fact that the greatest percentage of research in second language acquisition focuses on learners and learning (VanPatten and Benati 2010), and does not have any pedagogical implications, scholars often investigate the effectiveness of a particular theory, account or hypothesis in order to offer practical advice for second language teaching and language teachers. Research findings from classroom-based research, for instance, could lead to a revision of how best

Teachers should also be researchers.

Agree Disagree

Research is what teachers normally do in the classroom when they teach and evaluate.

Agree Disagree

Anybody can do research.

Agree Disagree

One way to understand research is to read a published paper and work out the structure of the paper.

Agree Disagree

Ideas for research come mainly from intuitions and personal interests.

Agree Disagree

Attending conferences is one key element to develop research ideas.

Agree Disagree

Figure 1.2 Evaluation of opinions about research

we teach languages. Second language research is conducted for a number of theoretical and empirical needs: the need to verify the nature and soundness of a theory which might lead to new insights; the need to discover the cause of a problem and find possible solutions; the need to monitor and influence the direction of new developments; the need to evaluate what is already taking place; and the need to find out what it is actually going on, recognizing that what actually occurs is not always the same as what is thought to occur.

Do you agree or disagree with the statement/assumptions shown in Figure 1.2?

1.2 Where Do Research Questions Come From?

Second language research is carried out for different purposes and it is generated from different sources. Scholars, teachers and students develop research ideas/questions from their own personal interests, ideas and intuitions or through reading relevant literature. Ideas for research come from

Note down full details of everything you read:
Author ....
Title ....
Date of publication ....
Publisher and place of publication ....
Key issues raised by the author relevant to the project ....
Methodology issues ....
Significance ....

Figure 1.3 Recording reading

many sources, such as thinking about our teaching, going to conferences, talking and listening to others, reading books and journals, becoming aware of a problem and taking courses. However, it is often not easy to formulate research questions. This is because sometimes as readers or researchers we focus on the findings of somebody's else research without fully understanding the process that the researcher went through to get the idea for it.

One way to begin thinking about research is to study the structure of published research. Although research papers are not exactly alike, there is a common structure used by scholars/writers which can be helpful in understanding the process used to generate research questions and carry out research. The question is: How can we get a research idea? Reading is a key component of developing a research project/idea. It involves the reading of published and unpublished materials such as books, chapters in books, journal articles, reports, conference papers and dissertations. It is vital that researchers read at the beginning, during and at the end of their project. At the beginning they read to check what other research has been done, to focus their ideas and to explore the context for their project. Reading at this stage needs to be contextualized so that researchers can generate researchable questions (see Section 1.3). Very often, good research ideas/questions are generated from problems mentioned by other researchers. During their research they read to keep up to date with developments, and to help them better understand the methods they are using and the field they are researching. It is crucial that researchers read about the specific subject as well as methodological issues. At the end of their research they read to see what impact their own work has had and to help develop ideas for further projects.

Researchers should record their reading in a methodical way (see the example in Figure 1.3) as this will help them to identify key relevant issues

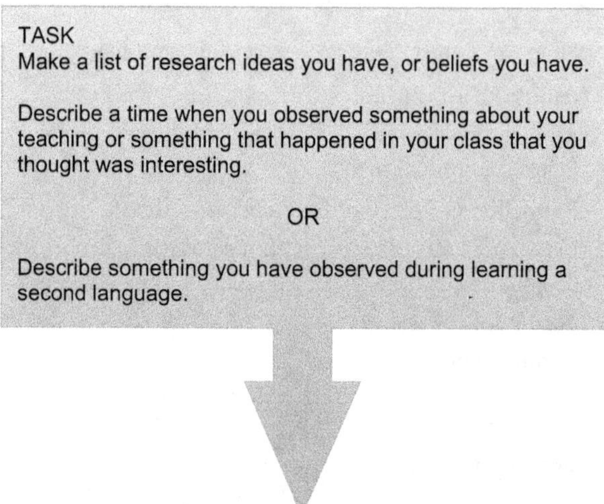

Figure 1.4 Task: Find ideas for research

for their project and write the literature review. There are a number of steps that a researcher can take to develop a research idea: discussing the idea with an instructor/supervisor; attending relevant conferences; and browsing relevant journals and periodicals. You should read edited volumes, monographs, journal articles, policy documents, academic papers, conference papers, dictionaries, encyclopaedias, etc. In locating the literature for your proposed research area you can do a search using an electronic database such as ERIC, MLA or Google Scholar.

The literature review is the first step to take in conducting a research project. First, it provides the reasons why the topic is of sufficient importance for it to be researched. Second, it provides the reader with a brief up-to-date account and discussion of literature on the issues relevant to the topic. Third, it provides a conceptual and theoretical context in which the topic for research can be situated. Fourth, it discusses relevant research carried out on the same topic or similar topics (see also Chapter 2).

1.3 What Is the Importance of the Research Plan?

In order to conduct second language research a careful plan needs to be developed and managed. This implies a process of organizing the elements or components of a research study. The lack of a coherent plan might have a devastating effect on the clarity of the project and the possibility of finding

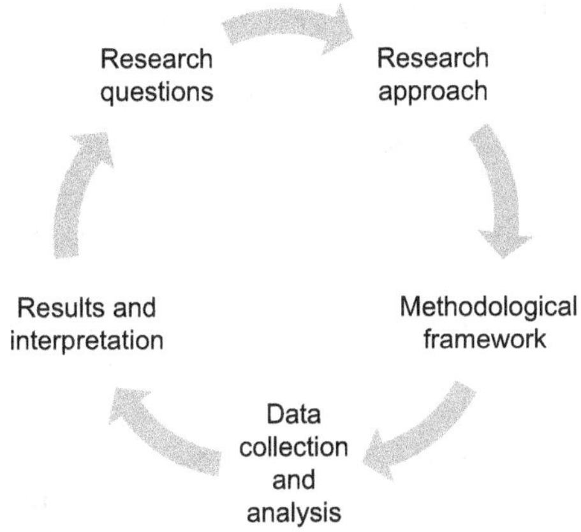

Figure 1.5 Research as a cyclical process

answers to the questions posed. Research is a scientific, methodical and disciplined inquiry. It is structured, organized and systematic. By designing a research project once the research question has been focused, a clear plan is needed. A coherent plan should clarify the focus of the researcher and should define main goals and questions. One of the main tasks to be addressed is the identification of the main variables involved in a study.

In the case of experimental design, the so-called independent variable is the factor manipulated by the researcher, and the dependent is the means by which any changes are measured. The effectiveness of a teaching approach (independent factor) is measured by testing learners' performance in an oral and written task (dependent factor).

Research as defined by Seliger and Shohamy (1989: 2) is cyclical. Research is a cyclical process which involves interrelated phases (see Figure 1.5). Initially, the researcher develops an interest. Reviewing the literature lead to the formulation questions and/or hypotheses. It provides the rationale or justification for doing the research. Then the researcher needs to establish what kind of data would provide the evidence to answer the questions or confirm the hypotheses of the proposed study. Therefore, a research design is chosen in relation to the specific problem to be investigated. An appropriate methodology (collection and data analysis) is chosen. Results are interpreted and summarized and related to the research questions and/or hypotheses raised at the beginning of the project. The main findings will provide possible answers to our initial questions and/or hypotheses. The answers obtained, however, do not close the research cycle, as other questions arise and further research avenues are always outlined.

1.3.1 Research Questions and/or Hypotheses

Producing feasible and important research questions and/or hypotheses is a key step in the research process. In second language research, questions and hypotheses are generated from a number of sources and from different research fields. Teachers' everyday experiences often provide the stimuli to generate questions. Curiosity about something observed in the classroom might motivate teachers and students to undertake a research project. For example, you might notice that students find it difficult to use the subjunctive. You then decide to investigate why they might be doing that. Reading other research in existing published and unpublished literature is also another key source to identify an interesting research question. All these different inputs might offer the stimulus for formulating a research question and/or hypothesis. The research question or research questions needs to be important and worth researching. This is usually called 'the research gap' and would help you to provide a rationale and justification for your research. It is also vital to be realistic about research question(s), as they need to be often answerable within a particular time period.

At the beginning of any research project a general research question is usually formulated. For example, you develop an interest in investigating the role of grammar instruction in second language learning. After reading some published materials the following research question is formulated: Does grammar instruction make a difference? The new researcher is interested in evaluating the role of grammar instruction in second language learning. A first analysis of this question reveals that it is too broad. The next step is for the researcher to break the question down and to narrow the scope of the research project. After contextualizing the reading, and reviewing relevant and specific aspects of the same area of enquiry (the role of grammar instruction), the researcher produces a more focused and researchable question: Would input enhancement affect the way English native speakers acquire Japanese passive constructions? (See Figure 1.6, which provides a flowchart for preparatory steps to be taken to narrow down an area of enquiry and formulate specific hypotheses or questions.)

Establishing 'theoretical importance' in a research project is one of the key components in the research process, as highlighted by Seliger and Shohamy (1989: 51). The importance of a question can be demonstrated through the literature review. Literature review provides the motivation and the background for a research project. It is necessary to acquire the general knowledge and eventually the very specific familiarity with the subject to be investigated in order to narrow down a general question to a researchable and focused question. This can be achieved by contextualizing and critically analyzing relevant

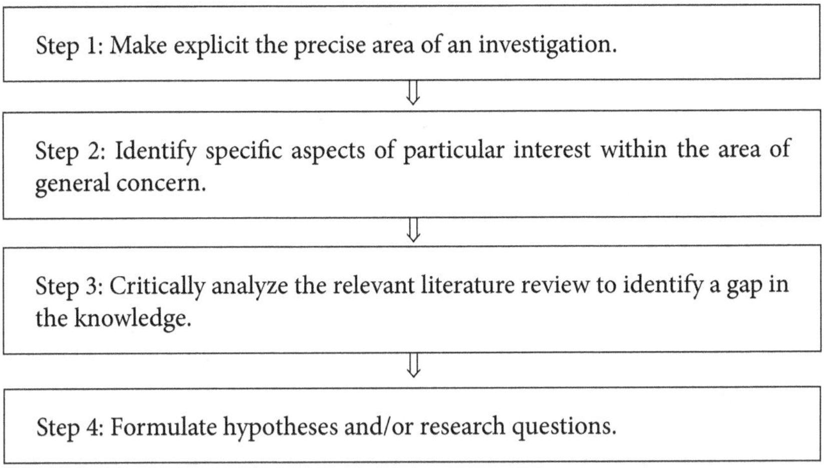

Step 1: Make explicit the precise area of an investigation.

⇓

Step 2: Identify specific aspects of particular interest within the area of general concern.

⇓

Step 3: Critically analyze the relevant literature review to identify a gap in the knowledge.

⇓

Step 4: Formulate hypotheses and/or research questions.

Figure 1.6 Preparatory steps

literature. This can be a difficult task because it is not always straightforward to know what to include and what to exclude in the literature review. In some cases, it is difficult to gather all the relevant sources. In other cases it is difficult to provide a 'critical angle' to the literature review. Establishing feasibility of a research project is also a difficult task. These are some of the questions which should be addressed at the initial stage of research to avoid having to abandon a study at a later stage due to unforeseen problems:

1. Are the terms and concepts used in the formulation of the general questions clearly defined? In order to avoid problems of ambiguity and inconsistency, the main terms of the research project should be clearly defined.
2. What logistical and practical problems can be anticipated? Any possible practical obstacle should be looked at in order to anticipate any possible problems arising from the study.

To summarize, the initial stage in second language research involves the identification of an area of enquiry by the researcher, and the formulation of a research question/hypothesis. Once an idea has been developed, the researcher, through the review of the relevant literature, will formulate important and researchable questions/hypotheses.

1.3.2 Research Approach

This stage involves the selection of the approach to the research project and the selection of participants, materials and overall methodological procedures. Once we have generated questions and/or hypotheses for our project, there are several possibilities in terms of research settings (natural or classroom settings) and research approaches (synthetic or analytic). The synthetic approach would view the research as a combination of factors to be analyzed. For example, classroom practice can be seen as an exercise made up of different parts (drill, tasks, group practice, pairs practice, etc.). To isolate one form from another may distort its role. Using this approach may allow the researcher to evaluate the relative contribution that each form of practice makes to the overall process of language learning. The analytic approach instead looks at one or some aspects in isolation and requires a clear definition of the terms which will become the focus of research (a specific construct to be investigated).

The researcher usually has two options in establishing the research approach to follow:

1. Developing an overall knowledge of the research subject and the phenomena under investigation and gathering data to learn more about this subject/these phenomena. This type of approach is inductive and descriptive in nature (see example below). The data obtained might generate a number of hypotheses and/or questions related to the phenomena observed.

   Example: Flyman-Mattsson (1999) conducted a study to provide a description of the communicativity in a foreign language classroom and also of students' communicative behaviour. In this study, different activities were observed and categorized with the intention of describing students' ability to communicate.
2. Developing a specific knowledge about a phenomenon and formulating hypotheses and questions based on previous research findings. The researcher will collect data to confirm or reject the hypotheses stated. This type of approach is deductive in nature (see example below).

   Example: Benati (2005) carried out a study to investigate the effects of an input-based approach to grammar instruction on the acquisition of the English past simple tense. Based on previous research findings it was hypothesized that this innovative approach to grammar instruction is more effective than traditional grammar instruction.

1.3.3 Research Design

Once a specific research approach for the research project has been chosen, consistent with the aims of the study, decisions have to be taken regarding which research design is the most appropriate and needs to be used to collect

Figure 1.7 Qualitative research

and analyze data. This stage requires the researcher to make decisions about what constitutes data and the type of data suitable for the research question to be investigated. The variables which need to be investigated in a given research study need to be identified and defined. Determining what constitutes data in second language research depends on the focus of the study and the specific variables which would have to be investigated. In Part Two of this book, a number of research frameworks (experimental, action research, classroom research observation and other qualitative frameworks) will be explored. Research designs are usually chosen on the basis of how best they address the purpose and the questions/hypotheses of a study. Types of data are usually described as qualitative or quantitative in nature (Creswell 2003, 2005). What does it mean?

Qualitative data usually derives from an observation of human behaviours in the natural context (see example below). It involves the study of the characteristics of a group in the real world with no manipulation. The analysis of the data leads the researcher to discover a number of phenomena such as patterns of learning behaviour. Common qualitative data collection instruments are: observations, interviews, questionnaires and diaries.

Example: Schmidt and Frota (1986) conducted a study on the development of conversational ability in Portuguese by one subject during five months in Brazil. The purpose of the study was twofold: to develop an understanding of the type and amount of language that was learned by the subject in order to communicate with native speakers; and to understand how both instruction and conversational interaction contributed to learning Portuguese. Journal entries and a diary were kept throughout the period of exposure to the language.

Qualitative research begins with an idea, and a methodology is developed to generate and analyze data. The analysis of the data should reveal a number of patterns from which a hypothesis and/or theory is induced (see Figure 1.7).

Quantitative data derives from controlled experimentation (see example below) conducted to investigate the possible relationship between two

Figure 1.8 Quantitative research

variables (treatment and the measurement of the treatment). It involves the formulation of questions/hypotheses beforehand. The analysis of the data provides an answer to the questions/hypotheses raised in the experiment. Common quantitative data collection instruments are tests and, in some cases, observation schemes.

Example: Ammar and Spada (2006) conducted a study investigating the relative effects of two corrective feedback techniques (recasts and prompts). Sixty-four students learning English were assigned to the three groups: two under experimental conditions – one received corrective feedback in the form of recasts and the other in the form of prompts – and one control group. The instructional lasted a period of four weeks and targeted the third-person English possessive determiners 'his' and 'her'. A pre-test/post-test procedure was adopted measuring immediate and delayed effects of instruction. The results of this study showed that prompts were more effective than recasts.

Quantitative research is based on an existing theory and empirical findings from which a hypothesis or a number of hypotheses are formulated. A methodology is developed and the data generated by the study are analyzed. The results obtained allow the researcher to deduce whether the hypothesis/hypotheses is/are true or wrong (see Figure 1.8).

Despite the difference in the two approaches (the choice is determined by the question the researcher is addressing), both qualitative and quantitative analysis can be applied to the same set of data. In the classroom transcript below (taken from Lightbown and Spada 1993: 74–75) it is clear that the teacher provides instruction which focuses on form (grammar). The only purpose of the interaction is to practise the present continuous. The teacher's goal is to make sure that students develop the ability to use the form correctly. An observer/researcher can identify some patterns in the interaction between the teacher (T) and the student (S). A qualitative analysis of the transcript, for example, would indicate the following: errors are few from the teacher and from the student, who doesn't say very much; errors are corrected by the teachers in a traditional fashion; there are no genuine questions from the students and few from the teacher related to classroom management; most of the questions from the teacher are display questions; there is very little negotiation of meaning in the interaction as the teacher focuses on the formal aspects of the language used by students, and students have no opportunity to determine the direction of the discourse.

T: OK, we finished the book – we finished in the book Units 1, 2, 3. Finished Workbooks 1, 2, 3. So today we're going to start with Unit 4. Don't take your books yet, don't take your books. In 1, 2, 3 we worked in what tense? What tense did we work on? OK?
S: Past
T: In the past – What auxiliary in the past?
S: Did
T: Did (writes on board '1-2-3 Past'). Unit 4, Unit 4, we're going to work in the present, present progressive, present continuous – OK? You don't know what it is?
S: Yes
T: Yes? What is it?
S: Little bit
T: A little bit
S: ...
T: Eh?
S: Uh, present continuous
T: Present continuous? What's that?
S: e-n-g
T: i-n-g
S: Yes
T: What does that mean, present continuous? You don't know? OK, fine. What are you doing, Paul?
S: Rien
T: Nothing?
S: Rien – nothing
T: You're not doing anything? You're doing *something*!
S: Not doing anything.
T: You're doing *something*!
S: Not doing anything.
T: You're doing *something* – Are, are you listening to me? Are you talking with Marc? What are you doing?
S: No, no – uh – listen – uh –
T: Eh?
S: To you
T: You're, you're listening to me.
S: Yes
T: Oh – (writes 'What are you doing? I'm listening to you' on the board).
S: Je –
T: What are you – ? You're excited.
S: Yes

T: You're playing with your eraser – (writes 'I'm playing with my eraser' on the board). Would you close the door please, Bernard? Claude, what is he doing?
S: Close the door
T: He is closing the door – (writes 'He's closing the door' on the board) What are you doing, Mario?
S: Moi, I listen to you.
T: You're listening to me.
S: Yes
T: OK. Are you sleeping or are you listening to me?
S: I don't – moitié-moitié, half and half.
T: Half and half, half sleeping, half listening.

(Transcripts from Lightbown and Spada 1993: 74–75)

A more quantitative analysis of the same transcript would try to support the hypothesis that the main purpose of the interaction is to practise the present continuous and the main goal for the teacher is to ensure that students develop the ability to use the form correctly, with numbers. Quantitative analysis can quantify the numbers of errors, feedback on errors, genuine and display questions and negotiation of meaning instances given by the teacher and the student. From Table 1.1, it could be concluded that the teacher is certainly in control of the interaction and its main purpose is to make sure that students use the form correctly. Statistical methods can be deployed to strengthen the argument.

The example provided illustrates how both qualitative and quantitative analysis can sometimes establish the how (qualitative) and how much (quantitative) of a phenomenon. Quantitative analysis is not only used for counting but also for comparing two or more groups of people or showing a possible relation between two or more factors.

Quantitative research addresses questions such as "What, exactly, is happening, and how often?", while qualitative research tries to find out "Why does it happen, and what do the people involved think about it?"

Table 1.1 Quantitative data

	Teacher	*Student*
Errors	0	2
Feedback on Errors	5	0
Genuine Questions	0	1
Display Questions	5	0
Negotiation of Meaning	0	0

Deciding on which approach to use is very much dependent on the purpose of the research and the kind of research question addressed.

Two key components of research designs are data collection procedures and data analysis procedures. The researcher needs to operationalize the main variables which are under investigation in a study. Specific behaviours would need to be identified, as these behaviours would provide evidence to describe the variables involved in the study. Once a decision is made on the data to collect, the next step is to decide how to collect them. In second language research, data are collected in a number of forms: observation schemes, questionnaires, interviews and tests (see Part Two for detailed examples of these data collection procedures). These data collection instruments produce data in two different forms: numbers and words. Scores in a test are quantitative data. Interviews from teachers or/and students are an example of qualitative data. Data collection through interviews produces words which need to be analyzed. Data must be analyzed and interpreted, and then requires some form of validation. There are usually two key terms related to validation: validity and reliability. Validity is the process of demonstrating the connection between the interpretation of the data/results and what it was originally intended to measure. Reliability refers to the process of demonstrating that results would be consistent from one data collection episode to another. Both constructs will be discussed in relation to the frameworks presented in this book.

Another main requirement, pointed out by Spada (1990), is that research designs should include both process (what is actually happening in the classroom) and product (what the learning outcomes are), with an observation component built in to verify the implementation of a particular method or technique. A final requirement is that research should be theoretically motivated in order to present a coherent view of the language teaching and language learning process. In the case of experimental research, for example, which is quantitative in nature, collection procedures involve numerical measurements and statistical analysis. However, despite the goal of this approach, a process dimension (classroom observation instrument) should be built into the experimental design to give a better account of the teaching and learning process.

1.3.4 Data Collection Instruments and Data Analysis

Data are a crucial element for any research as they allow the researcher to make objective and scientific claims about a phenomenon. Data collection instruments include, among others, observation schemes, questionnaires, tests, interviews and psycholinguistic methods (self-paced reading, eye-tracking methods, etc.). These instruments produce qualitative (transcripts, answers/views from a questionnaire or interview, notes from observation, etc.) and/or quantitative data (scores from a test) to be analyzed and then interpreted by the researcher. Data collection instruments require validation to be used in scientific research (see the section on reliability and validity in this chapter). It must be said that even if certain collection procedures are more appropriate for certain methodological frameworks (e.g. observation schemes are normally used in the observation research framework and tests in the experimental research framework), researchers often make use of different collection procedures. There are a number of possible methodologies (qualitative, quantitative or mixed methods) together with a variety of data collection instruments (e.g. questionnaire, tests, interviews, etc.).

Observation Schemes

Observation schemes, as a data collection research tool, are perhaps one of the oldest methods used to collect data in the language classroom. The rationale behind the use of this instrument to collect data is to provide detailed and precise information about what goes on in the language classroom, and it is used in second language research for various purposes.

Observation is the act of watching something and recording the results in a way that produces data that can be analyzed and interpreted (Nunan 1992). Observation approaches can be open or closed. Open observations do not require observers to specify in advance what they intend to look at or record. 'Open' means that the observers are interested in what is happening, but they have not determined exactly what they intend to observe. The observer writes in-class observation notes. 'Closed observation' means that the observers have decided what they intend to observe. The data gathered may be quantitative, such as frequency counts, or qualitative, such as verbal descriptions. A type of closed observation is a checklist, which is a form with predetermined or closed categories, usually listed down one side of the page. Space is provided (often in little boxes) to mark the presence or absence of the predetermined category. The resulting data are frequency data. Structured observation is another form of closed classroom observation using previously defined categories. In some cases, an observation form is given to the observer, with instructions to note when, how often, or examples of classroom activities that in the observer's opinion exemplify the category.

Although it was always considered a major way of collecting qualitative data, it has also been used in quantitative and more experimental research

Time	Activities	Partic. Organization							Content							
		Class			Group		Indiv.		Man		Language				Other Topics	
		T s/c	S s/c	Choral	Same	Different	Same	Different	Procedure	Discipline	Form	Function	Discourse	Socioling.	Narrow	Broad

Content Control			Student Modality					Materials							
								Type				Source			
Teacher	Teacher/Stud.	Student	Listening	Speaking	Reading	Writing	Other	Minimal	Extended	Audio	Visual	L2-NNS	L2-NS	L2-NSA	Student-made

Figure 1.9 COLT Part A (adapted from Spada 1990)

study. This is the case of a structured observation scheme called COLT (Communicative Orientation of Language Teaching, see Spada 1990). COLT (see Figure 1.9), which was developed to measure the communicative orientation of language classrooms, captures the main characteristics of the communicative language teaching approach. COLT has two parts: part A describes a classroom event at the level of classroom tasks and activities; and part B analyzes the communicative features of verbal interactions between instructors and students in classroom activities. This observation scheme includes five major categories (Spada 1990): activity type (type of tasks learners are required to do); participant organization (type of interaction); content (type of instruction, meaning-based or form-based in its orientation); student modality (time spent on developing the four skills); materials (type, length and source of materials used). Each of these categories is divided into subcategories designed to describe categories of classroom procedures based on communicative language teaching theoretical and pedagogical approach. COLT describes differences in the kind of instruction students receive in the language classroom. The classroom is observed by an investigator and all the activities are coded and subsequently analyzed. In order to establish differences among groups in the categories considered, the analysis involves the calculation of the amount of time spent by teachers and students on the various categories and subcategories of the observation scheme. By following this analysis procedure, percentages are obtained for the various categories of the scheme.

Example: An experiment is conducted to establish possible instructional differences among three groups learning Japanese at intermediate level. The three groups have been instructed using the same communicative programme. The data are collected by an observer through the use of COLT part A in three classrooms for four weeks. The results of the analysis indicate that the three classes are similar in most features. For example, in the case of the participant organization category, the analysis shows that instruction is teacher-centred for 50% of the time for all classes. Similarly, in terms of the student modality category, the three classes spend most of their time primarily listening to the teacher or other students (45% of the time). However, some of the results of the data analysis show some important instructional differences among the three groups. For instance, in the case of the content category, although the three classes spent most of the time (50%) focusing exclusively on meaning-based activities and less time on form-based activities, the analysis shows that there are some individual group differences in the amount of time spent on form-based instruction (group one 32%; group two 22%; group three 9%). Based on these findings, the researcher hypothesized that this particular instructional difference might have a direct effect on the three groups' learning outcomes.

The analysis can be qualitative or quantitative as in the case of structured observation schemes. Observations are often recorded. Observation schemes and techniques will be presented and discussed in more detail in Chapter 4.

Questionnaires

Questionnaires are often used to collect data on phenomena not easily observed, such as attitudes or motivation (see Dörnyei and Taguchi 2010). They are more generally used to collect data on all processes involved in

1.	Name:	2.	Nationality:
3.	Mother tongue:	4.	Age:
5.	Sex:	6.	Degree course:
7.	Previous study or knowledge of Italian: yes no If yes, what kind?		
8.	Other foreign languages you know or you are studying:		
9.	Do you have any qualification in a foreign language? If yes, what mark did you get?		
10.	Do you use Italian in any way with someone outside the classroom?		
11.	Do you have any contact with native speakers outside the classroom?		
12.	Have you ever visited Italy? If yes, how long for?		

Figure 1.10 Background questionnaire

learning and using languages, and also to obtain background information (see Figure 1.10.) Background questionnaires could provide information on the following: background information; quality and quantity of the learner's previous exposure to different types of foreign language learning; learners' attitudes to the different language-teaching methods already experienced; and learner's expectations, attitudes and degree of motivation to learn a language.

A questionnaire is often seen as a number of questions related to a specific area of enquiry (Dörnyei and Taguchi 2010). A questionnaire can be administered in different ways: pencil-and-paper form; online form; email form; or telephone form. Questionnaires are often paper- or computer-based instruments asking respondents for their opinions, as opposed to measuring learning performance. Questionnaires comprise three sections: demographics; closed-ended items; and open-ended items. At the beginning the researcher needs to develop a section which contains the title of the questionnaire, the date, the name and other general information about the respondent. Typically, a questionnaire is then formatted following two options: closed-ended and open-ended. A closed-ended questionnaire either asks the questionnaire-taker, called a *respondent*, to make a choice between two options, or alternatively it asks the respondent to choose an option that

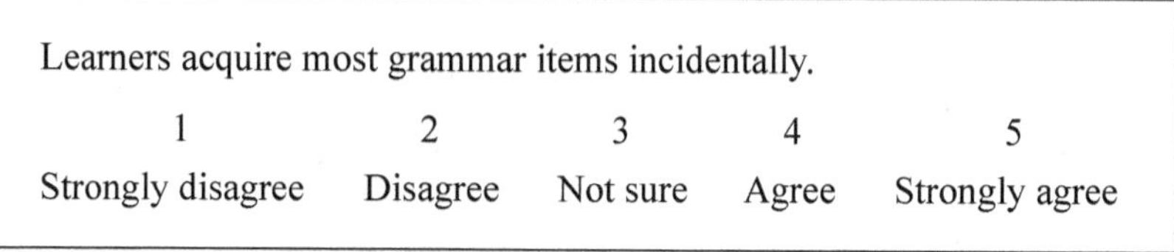

Learners acquire most grammar items incidentally.

1	2	3	4	5
Strongly disagree	Disagree	Not sure	Agree	Strongly agree

Figure 1.11 Questionnaire using Likert scale

What do you think would be the best way to teach grammar?

Write your answer below.

____

Figure 1.12 Open-ended item

in some way produces a number. As a result, closed-ended items are often easier and faster to answer than open-ended items. Examples might include true and false and Likert scale items (see Figure 1.11).

An open-ended item is one that requires the respondent to express an opinion about a topic in direct response to a question (Figure 1.12). Questionnaire designers must decide which type of item to include.

Data from closed-ended items are usually drawn from a scale that quantifies the data. Depending on the scale used, this can mean frequency data (how many or how often); dichotomous data (true or false); ordinal data (ranking); or continuous data (such as Likert scales), often on a 1–5 scale. Numerical data can be analyzed statistically to show trends or patterns ranging from simple percentages to descriptive statistics including mean and standard deviation. Data from open-ended items are qualitative (words). Researchers take a number of steps to analyze this type of data. First, they transcribe the data, probably into an editable document for easy manipulation. Second, they think about how they intend to use the data, and they group them accordingly. For example, if they posed their open-ended items to investigate A, B and C, then they group the transcribed data responses into three groups named A, B and C. Third, they read what they have grouped together, looking for key ideas (patterns, common views ...). Fourth, they read the key ideas/opinions again to see if they can identify recurring themes. Finally, for each theme they select a response that exemplifies the theme. More detailed information and discussion about questionnaires will be provided in Chapter 5 of this book.

Tests

Tests are an instrument used to collect data about the subjects' knowledge of a second language in areas such as vocabulary, grammar, language skills, metalinguistic awareness and general proficiency. Tests are considered dependent factors in second language research and are often used to measure the effects of an independent factor, which is usually a teaching method or a teaching technique.

Example: An experiment is carried out to investigate the effects of two different instructional grammar techniques (innovative vs traditional) in the acquisition of English past forms. Two tests are developed for this study (listening test and writing tests). The listening test is constructed as a comprehension test as it consists of 10 sentences (five target forms in the past tense and five off-target forms in the present tense). Test-takers would need to establish whether the sentence refers to an action in the past or in the present by relying on the verb ending. If they are not sure they could tick the option "not sure" (see Figure 1.13). The scoring are calculated as follows: incorrect response = 0 points; correct response = 1 point.

Listen to each statement about your teacher and decide whether he does them now or last weekend. If you are not sure, please tick the option 'Not sure'.

Now	Last weekend	Not sure
❑	❑	❑
❑	❑	❑
❑	❑	❑
❑	❑	❑
❑	❑	❑
❑	❑	❑

Sentences heard by learners

1. .... played tennis in the park with his friends
2. .... corrects exams
3. .... cooked Italian food
4. .... watched the football match
5. .... teaches a class

(The activity continues in a similar fashion)

Figure 1.13 Interpretation test

> You should fill the gaps with the right verb ending (10 gaps)
>
> Yesterday, John ________ (phone) his girlfriend Mary and they ________ (talk) together for about one hour. Mary ________ (want) to play tennis later that day. John quickly ________ (brush) his teeth and ________ (dress) in his white T-shirt and shorts. At 1pm he ________ (walk) to the tennis courts to meet Mary. They ________ (play) together for about two hours and ________ (enjoy) themselves a lot. Afterwards, they ________ (watch) a movie together. Later at John's house he ________ (cook) a meal for Mary. Unfortunately, the food was terrible and Mary was sick!

Figure 1.14 Production test

The writing test is constructed as a sentence-completion production test in order to measure learners' ability to produce correct forms in the past tense (see Figure 1.14) which test-takers need to complete. The scoring procedure is the same as the listening test. Based on the statistical analysis of the two groups' scores the researchers conclude that the innovative approach is more effective than the traditional approach in improving learners' performance on both interpretation and production of sentences containing the target feature.

Statistical analyses are used to compare the performance of two groups in a test. Statistical analysis helps to determine that difference between two or more groups is not due to chance. Two types of analysis are normally used: descriptive and parametric. Descriptive statistics are used to calculate the average (mean) and range (standard deviation) of the score for each group under investigation. Parametric statistics consists of a number of procedures to measure statistical relevance between and within a dependent and an independent factor. The procedure used to compare two groups is called a *t*-test. The statistical procedure used to compare more than two groups is called ANOVA.

All tests need to be thoroughly evaluated before they are used. The discussion of tasks and criteria for assessment is in fact a key contribution to achieve valid and reliable testing procedure. Reliability can be defined as consistency of measurement and is a measure of the degree to which a test gives the same results when it is given on different occasions or when different people use it. Below is a list that researchers need to consider to make their test reliable:

1. Take enough samples of behaviour.
2. Do not allow participants too much freedom.
3. Write unambiguous items.
4. Ensure that tests are well laid out and perfectly legible.
5. Candidates should be familiar with format and testing techniques.
6. Provide uniform and non-distracting conditions of administration.
7. Develop detailed scoring procedures.

Tests will be discussed in more details in Chapter 3 of this book.

Interviews

In an interview the researcher asks a number of questions to collect the views and opinions of the interviewee. A so-called open interview allows the respondent wide latitude in how to answer. An example is: What is your view about grammar instruction? Open interviews are normally used when the approach to the research is qualitative and the research's intention is to explore more general phenomena. A closed interview asks all respondents the same factual questions, in the same order, using the same words. Closed interviews are normally used in quantitative studies when researchers have developed a number of hypotheses they want to confirm or reject.

In order to develop an interview there are various issues that need to be considered. First of all, the type of interview that best suits the purpose of the research project should be chosen. Second, the audience/population to interview should be selected and consideration should be given to how many respondents should be interviewed. Third, the questions should be formulated. There are a number of questions that can be asked in an interview: questions to gauge people's previous experience; questions to elicit opinions about a particular issue; questions to find out what people know; background questions such as gender, age, previous knowledge about something, etc. Fourth, how the data should be collected and analyzed should be decided. There are two main approaches:

1. Extrapolating categories from the data as the researcher becomes familiar with the data and there is an attempt to interpret what the respondent is talking about. Categories emerge from the data and reflect the data. The researcher does not impose anything but lets the data speak to him.

Step one: Listen to the recording and transcribe the interview.

Step two: Read the transcripts several times to familiarize yourself with what is being said.

Step three: Code the interview. Coding entails reading the transcript until certain themes become apparent. Identify each theme with a short word or phrase. This word or short phrase is the code. After you have your codes, define them so you can be consistent in coding across multiple interviews.

Step four: Write a summary of the coded data. For example, on a piece of paper (or word processing document) write the code, and under each code list what the respondent said. For example, under the code 'grammar' you might put two comments, one of which is 'Grammar is the main context of the course.' Under the code block you might put seven comments, one of which is 'Course grammar book not related to academic writing.' In this way several pages of transcribed interview data are reduced down to one and a half pages of comments under various codes.

Step five. Write a memo to yourself that not only summarizes but ties together all the content.

Figure 1.15 Steps used to analyze interviews

2. Creating categories before the interview takes place. The researcher does not ask questions randomly but rather has a clear idea of what and why he/she is asking certain questions.

There are a number of steps that need to be taken to analyze an interview (see Figure 1.15).

More examples of interviews and how to develop and analyze them will be presented and discussed in Chapter 6 of this book.

1.3.5 Results and Interpretation

This process involves the interpretation of the results in the light of the research questions/hypotheses raised. In this phase the researcher's intention is to report and summarize research results but also to identify the

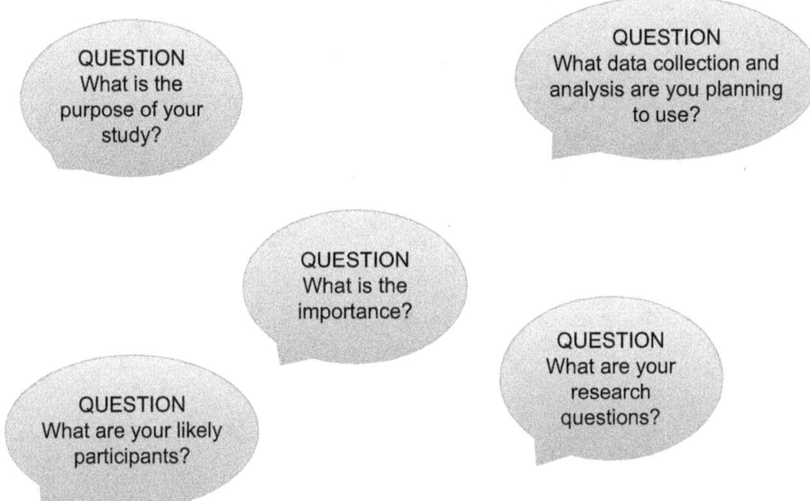

Figure 1.16 Questions

implications of the results and recommend possible further research avenues. The main stages involved in this final phase are: reporting, summarizing and interpreting the results. In the reporting and summarizing stages, the researcher reports the results obtained in the study through the analysis techniques which have been used. At this stage, the use of tables, charts, category lists or graphs to present data are an effective way to present main findings clearly. In the interpretation phase, a more in-depth analysis of the results is provided. This section goes beyond the simple presentation of the main outcomes of the study and provides a more detailed discussion of the significance of the results in relation to more specific theoretical and practical issues related the research undertaken. The researcher also discusses the meaning of the research results and places them in a broader and general context. It identifies a number of implications at theoretical and pedagogical level and also recommends different applications of the research findings and indicates possible new areas of research. All the discussion issues, reflections and recommendations made are linked to the context in which the research was originally conducted. Research is a cyclical process formed by a sequence of events (see Figure 1.5) which leads the researcher back to the starting point, as research findings ought to provide an answer to the questions/hypotheses raised. However, in the nature of research the more answers are obtained, the more questions usually arise, leading other researchers to undertake new research in the field.

TASK
Choose a couple of studies in second language research and identify the following:
- Research questions/hypotheses
- Research approach
- Design
- Data collection procedures and analysis
- Results

Figure 1.17 Task

1.3.6 Validity and Reliability

Validity in second language research refers to the ability of the researchers to develop tools which measure what exactly it is intended to measure. Research tools to measure learners' attitude, motivation (questionnaires) or performance (tests) must be designed with measurement validity in mind. Only planning and preparation can help the researcher to address validity issues and minimize possible methodological problems (see next chapters for more specific information and definition of validity). The researcher must ensure that the collection instruments are validated.

Reliability in research refers to the ability to deploy a methodology/methodological tool that measures consistently and accurately a phenomenon and obtains the same results if the same participants, environment and circumstances are in place and are tested. In second language research it is often very difficult to have access to an identical population and environment. Nevertheless, methodological tools used in research to measure the effects of certain variables (clearly defined) must be reliable. Other researchers using the same tools in their investigations should be able to obtain the same results and data. Checking a method's reliability can be accomplished using two main procedures: split-half method and test-retest method. In the first case, the population sample is randomly split into two equal groups. If the methodological tools are reliable, the method administered to the two groups should provide equal results for both groups. In the case of the second procedure, the sample of the population is used (not split) and methodological instruments are tested at two different points in time. If the results are the same or very similar, reliability for the methodological tools is ensured.

Establishing reliability and validity in second language research does not necessarily require large-scale statistical investigations, as very often crucial insights into language learning and teaching processes are obtained through small-scale research projects. However, there are two important elements which need to be considered when embarking on a research project: triangulation and saturation. The idea of triangulation is to examine a phenomenon from several different points of view/angles and by using different data collection techniques (a test and a questionnaire, for example). Choosing particular techniques will depend on the question under investigation, but in many cases both qualitative and quantitative procedures can be used. The use of different procedures to collect data would increase accuracy in the data collected. Researchers also use triangulation to validate data collection instruments. There are a number of triangulation procedures to verify and validate instruments: measuring consistency of findings by using different data collection instruments; using multiple analysts to review findings; and interpreting the data using a variety of theoretical perspectives.

Saturation refers to the opportunity of repeating the data collection over a period of time, or continuing it for as long as possible to ensure that the results are not due to chance. Second language research needs to demonstrate that particular patterns of behaviour are typical and standard. The only way to do this is through replications and repetitions of the same study and the data collection.

1.3.7 Pulling It All Together

This is the final stage of a research project/study. The purpose of the study, the question(s), the design, the results obtained and a reflection and interpretation of the main findings all need to be pulled together. The project structure includes the following sections:

Introduction
Theoretical Background
Design
Results
Conclusion
Bibliography
Appendices

The introduction is usually written at the end of the project and introduces the reader to the key aspects of the project (scope, significance, main questions to be addressed). The Theoretical Background is the section where the researcher reviews the previous research and theory and establishes the motivation of the study by formulating specific questions/hypotheses. In the design session, the methods used by the researcher for its investigation are presented. Common components of this section are: description of the population, data collection procedures and data analysis procedures. The results section normally consists of a summary statement of the research results obtained and then a discussion of their meaning. In the conclusion section the writer summarizes the possible contribution(s) of the results to the general area of research, their implications and whether these results can lead to recommendations and suggestions for further research. The bibliography contains the sources and references used and consulted, while the appendices include additional material used, tests, raw data, questionnaires or any other procedures used which are too detailed to be included in the main body of the research report.

1.4 What Are the Main Ethical Issues?

Researchers, students, lecturers and teachers often need to address ethical issues in their research (Oliver 2010). Universities and educational institutions have developed research ethics policies regarding research which include all human participation, whether in the form of "interviews, questionnaires, surveys, observation" or any other direct contact. It is required that all participants must consent to taking part in a study before the beginning of the data collection phase. In most cases written consent from the participants must be obtained. Participants must be made aware of possible risks that might be involved in the study and have the right to withdraw from the study at any time. They need to be informed of the use that the researcher might make of the data collected and must sign a consent form. Completing an ethical form is also a legal requirement. Researchers and students would normally need to obtain ethical approval from the Research Ethics Committee by supplying sufficient information on the experiment/data collection proposed.

This must include the following:

- outline of the project: what you want to do and what the rationale behind it is;
- information about the researcher (ability and skills necessary for conducting the proposed study);
- plan of how the study will be conducted;
- information about the participants (potential harm the study might have on them);
- information about data gathering;

- consent form for participants;
- how data collected will be used and kept;
- risk and risk management.

Researchers must make sure that all participants and stakeholders are reassured that all information and data will remain confidential and anonymous. They need to explain the various steps undertaken to ensure that participants' anonymity is secured and records of the experiment will be kept in a specific location where only a few people will have access to them.

Participants will be asked to fill a consent form (see Figure 1.18) prior to the beginning of data collection. If the participant is under age, the parent or guardian will normally complete the form.

- I have read the Participant Information Sheet about this study.
- I have had an opportunity to ask questions and discuss this study.
- I have received satisfactory answers to all my questions.
- I have received enough information about this study.
- I understand that I am/the participant is free to withdraw from this study:
  - At any time (until such date as this will no longer be possible, which I have been told).
  - Without giving a reason for withdrawing.
  - (If I am/the participant is, or intends to become, a student at the University of Greenwich) without affecting my/the participant's future with the University.
  - Without affecting any medical or nursing care I/the participant may be receiving.
- I understand that my research data may be used for a further project in anonymous form, but I am able to opt out of this if I so wish, by ticking here.
- I agree to take part in this study.

Signature (participant):	Date
Name in block letters:	
Signature (parent/guardian/other, if under 18):	Date
Name in block letters:	
Signature of researcher:	Date
This project is supervised by:	
Researcher's contact details (including telephone number and email address):	

Figure 1.18 Consent form

Another important ethical aspect, additional to the participants' rights and welfare, is to ensure universities and other higher or further education institutions of the personal security and safety of the research staff or research student undertaking the study. Particularly in the case of travelling to another institution or another country to collect data, the researcher and supervisor must reassure the Research Ethics Committee about the safety of the researcher. A consent form must be obtained from the institution from where the data will be collected.

1.5 What Are the Key Terms?

Qualitative describes a research framework which observes human behaviour in the natural context.

Quantitative is a term used in experimental controlled design where the strengths of the relationship between variables are quantified.

Questionnaires are often paper- or computer-based instruments asking respondents for their opinions, as opposed to measuring learning.

Questions make explicit the precise area of an investigation, identify specific aspects of particular interest within the area of general concern, guide you toward the kind of information you need and the ways you should collect the information, and help researchers to analyze the information you have collected.

Hypothesis is a tentative proposition which is subject to verification through subsequent investigation. In many cases hypotheses are hunches that the researcher has about the existence of a relationship between variables.

Interviews are usually one-to-one face-to-face meetings in which the data-gatherer asks questions to someone being interviewed.

Observation is the act of watching something and recording the results in a way that produces data that can be analyzed and interpreted.

Tests judge actual experiences of persons doing tasks that they are likely to do in real life.

Triangulation is an approach to data collection from different perspectives. It involves the use of different qualitative and quantitative data collection procedures (interviews and tests for example).

1.6 What Are the Key Readings?

Brown, J.D., & Rodgers, T. (2002). *Doing Second Language Research*. Oxford: Oxford University.

Creswell, J. (2003). *Research Design: Qualitative, Quantitative, and Mixed Methods Approaches* (2nd ed.). Thousands Oaks, CA: SAGE.

Creswell, J. (2005). *Educational Research: Planning, Conducting, and Evaluating Quantitative and Qualitative Research* (2nd ed.). Upper Saddle River, NJ: Merrill Prentice Hall.

Dörnyei, Z. (2007). *Research Methods in Applied Linguistics*. New York, NY: Oxford University Press.

Dörnyei, Z., & Taguchi, T. (2010). *Questionnaires in Second Language Research. Construction, Administration, and Processing*. New York: Routledge.

Gass, S., & Mackey, A. (2005). *Second Language Research. Methodology and Design*. Mahwah, NJ: Lawrence Erlbaum Associates.

Jegerski, J., & VanPatten, B. (2014). *Research Methods in Second Language Psycholinguistics*. New York, NY: Routledge.

Litosseliti, L. (2009). *Research Methods in Linguistics*. London: Continuum.

Mackey, A., & Gass, S. (Eds.). (2012). *Research Methods in Second Language Acquisition: A Practical Guide*. Malden, MA: Wiley–Blackwell.

McKay, S. (2006). *Research Second Language Classrooms*. Mahwah, NJ: Lawrence Erlbaum Associates.

Nunan, D. (1989). *Understanding Language Classrooms: A Guide for Instructor-initiated Action*. New York, NY: Prentice-Hall.

Nunan, D. (1992). *Research Methods in Language Learning*. Cambridge: Cambridge Language Teaching Library.

Oliver, P. (2010). *The Student's Guide to Research Ethics*. Maidenhead: Open University Press.

Rasinger, S. (2013). *Quantitative Research in Linguistics*. London: Bloomsbury.

Richards, K., Ross, S., & Seedhouse, P. (2012). *Research Methods for Applied Language Studies*. New York, NY: Routledge.

Seliger, H., & Shohamy, E. (1989). *Second Language Research Methods*. Oxford: Oxford University Press.

Wei, L., & Moyer, M. (Eds.). (2008). *The Blackwell Guide to Research Methods in Bilingualism and Multilingualism*. Oxford: Blackwell.

2 What Are the Key Components of a Typical Research Paper?

Chapter Preview

In this chapter, the format of the standard research paper will be presented and discussed. Even though every research paper is unique in content and structure, there is an organizational pattern that writers/researchers tend to follow and it is considered typical and standard. One experimental study (Benati, Lee, and Hikima 2010) and one case study (Nabei and Swain 2002) will be used to provide examples and to illustrate how these components are included in a paper from two different research frameworks.

2.1 What Are the Key Components of a Research Paper?

Findings from research projects in second language learning and teaching are often published in academic journals such as *Language Learning*, *Studies in Second Language Acquisition*, *Second Language Research*, *Language Awareness*, *Applied Linguistics*, *Language Teaching Research* and *Modern Language Journal*. A research project provides an opportunity for the researcher to undertake a study in depth, to extend an understanding of the theoretical and practical basis of a specific area and topic, to demonstrate the ability to reflect and conduct a study on a specific area, and to show awareness of potential and limitations of the research framework chosen. A typical research paper would include the following components:

Title
Abstract
Background
Design

Results
Discussion/Conclusion
References/Appendices

2.1.1 Title

The title of a paper is important, as very often potential readers will decide whether or not to read a paper from the title. Also, deciding on a title that appropriately describes the specific research topic in full is advantageous for a number of reasons:

- The research paper will be in a number of specific databases and it will be easier for readers to conduct a database search.
- The research paper will be located in a particular area of enquiry and it will be easier to find the paper for literature review purposes.

From the title, we can establish the nature and the keywords of the research undertaken and presented (see examples in Figure 2.1).

2.1.2 Abstract

The abstract usually provides a synthesis of research presented in the paper (see an example in Figure 2.2) or in a conference paper. It is often a short summary (about 100 to 200 words) and must include the following information: purpose of the research; research design utilized; summary of the main findings; and implications (theoretical, pedagogical and/or methodological) for the particular field.

> An experimental study into the effects of processing instruction on discourse-level interpretation tasks with the Japanese passive construction.
>
> Learner awareness of recasts in classroom interaction: a case study of an adult EFL student's second language learning.

Figure 2.1 Titles

> The main aim of the present study was to explore the effects of processing instruction as measured by discourse-level interpretation tasks. However, the research presented in this paper has a connection with previous research on processing instruction and therefore measurements for interpretation and production sentence-level tasks were also included. The study focuses on a linguistic item of the Japanese language not previously investigated: passive forms. A set of four research questions were formulated:
>
> Q1. Would learners receiving processing instruction improve in their ability to interpret sentences containing Japanese passive forms?
>
> Q2. Would learners receiving processing instruction improve in their ability to produce sentences containing Japanese passive forms?
>
> Q3. Would learners receiving processing instruction improve in their ability to interpret discourse, as measured by a guided recall of a dialogue containing Japanese passive forms?
>
> Q4. Would learners receiving processing instruction improve in their ability to interpret discourse, as measured by a guided recall of a story containing Japanese passive forms?

Figure 2.2 Abstract (adapted sample from Benati, Lee, and Hikima 2010)

2.1.3 Background

The background section is normally used by the writer to achieve two things: to state the importance of the topic investigated in a specific area of inquiry; and to identify a problem or gap in the research field and indicate the purpose of the study. Research projects are normally aimed at filling gaps in the knowledge of a particular area of research, raising a number of questions for which an answer must be provided, and confirming or refuting a claim already made by another researcher.

First, a statement of the problem is provided, where the writer emphasizes why the research is important in a specific field. An example from an experimental study (Benati, Lee, and Hikima 2010: 148) is: "The findings of research investigating the effects of processing instruction has provided unanimous support for this psycholinguistically motivated input-based approach to grammar instruction. The research findings indicate that not only is processing instruction an effective approach to grammar instruction, but that, in the majority of studies, it is more effective than other instructional approaches (e.g. traditional

> The main aim of the present study was to explore the effects of processing instruction as measured by discourse-level interpretation tasks. However, the research presented in this paper has a connection with previous research on processing instruction and therefore measurements for interpretation and production sentence-level tasks were also included. The study focuses on a linguistic item of the Japanese language not previously investigated: passive forms. A set of four research questions were formulated:
>
> Q1. Would learners receiving processing instruction improve in their ability to interpret sentences containing Japanese passive forms?
>
> Q2. Would learners receiving processing instruction improve in their ability to produce sentences containing Japanese passive forms?
>
> Q3. Would learners receiving processing instruction improve in their ability to interpret discourse, as measured by a guided recall of a dialogue containing Japanese passive forms?
>
> Q4. Would learners receiving processing instruction improve in their ability to interpret discourse, as measured by a guided recall of a story containing Japanese passive forms?

Figure 2.3 Purpose of a research paper (experimental study)

instruction, meaning output-based instruction)." An example from a case study (Nabei and Swain 2002: 43) is: "The recast and its role as corrective feedback is a controversial issue among second language acquisition (SLA) researchers. Although it appears a simple and straightforward behaviour, recasting is a complex activity, the interpretation of which is influenced by discourse contexts (e.g. Oliver, 1995) and people's intentions."

Second, the writer must elaborate on how the proposed paper might make a key contribution in the field and might address a gap in the existing knowledge. An example from an experimental study is: "Very little research has explored the effects of processing instruction on discourse level tasks" (Benati, Lee, and Hikima 2010: 148). An example from a case study design is: "As discussed in the following literature review, more data are required to understand, in particular, learners' cognitive activities when they receive feedback" (Nabei and Swain 2002: 143).

Third, the writer states the purpose of the research paper. The first example is from an experimental study design (see Figure 2.3, adapted from Benati, Lee, and Hikima 2010: 149).

> The present case study of a L2 learner, Shoko, was conducted to investigate this Japanese EFL college student's awareness of recast feedback provided by the teacher in a theme-based English classroom. The main concern of the study was to explore the following:
>
> - How recast was provided.
> - What Shoko learned from recast.
> - How Shoko reacted to recast.
>
> Shoko's awareness – often not observable in her behaviour in the class – was elicited through stimulated recall. Specifically, the research questions addressed in this study were:
>
> 1. What opportunities did Shoko have to hear recasts from the teacher?
> 2. What was Shoko's awareness of the teacher's recasts?
> 3. What connections are there among the teacher recasts, Shoko's awareness and her learning?

Figure 2.4 Purpose of a research paper (case study)

The next example (adapted from Nabei and Swain 2002: 47) is from a case study (see Figure 2.4).

The literature review is a key component of the background section. It is the section in the research paper where the researcher establishes the main purpose of the study and formulates the research questions. The literature review is a report on the theory and research evidence relevant to the problem (focusing on different aspects of the problem). In the literature review the researcher provides a conceptual and theoretical context in which the topic for research can be situated. In the description of the literature the researcher focuses on the theoretical claims made in the research. A survey of findings is made, particularly the major findings of the relevant studies, with a discussion of how they were obtained and what can be learned from them, particularly in relation to the specific research we want to conduct. An important part of the literature review (see Figure 2.5) is the critique of the research studies, pointing out problems in design, argumentation, analysis and conclusions.

The review of previous empirical and theoretical research normally leads to a number of research questions formulated by the writer/researchers at the end of the background section.

- To give reasons why the topic is of sufficient importance for it to be researched.
- To provide the reader with a brief up-to-date account and discussion of literature on the issues relevant to the topic.
- To provide a conceptual and theoretical context in which the topic for research can be positioned.
- To discuss relevant research carried out on the same topic or similar topics.

Figure 2.5 Key components of the literature review

An effective literature review must provide the reader with a logical and original synthesis of previous research leading to a number of questions and hypotheses. Through a question the researcher makes explicit the precise area of an investigation, and identifies specific aspects of particular interest within the area of general concern. A hypothesis is a tentative proposition which is subject to verification through subsequent investigation. In many cases hypotheses are hunches that the researcher has about the existence of a relationship between two or more variables. To summarize, a background section will include the following:

Statement of the problem
Purpose of the paper (significance of the study)
Literature review
Research questions

In other words, the background is the section where the writer talks about the 'what' and the 'why' of a particular study.

2.1.4 Design

The design used for a research project is normally presented in detail so that the reader has a very clear idea of the method and procedure used by the researcher to investigate the research problem (questions/hypotheses), collect the data and draw some conclusion on the main research findings. Common components of this section are:

1. description of the participants involved in the project (participants):
2. information on the overall procedure adopted;

3. procedures used to collect data (e.g. materials, assessments, scoring, etc.) and procedures used to analyze data (e.g. statistical analysis, qualitative measures to analyze data, etc.).

This is the part of the research paper where the writer explains 'how' the study has been conducted. Normally, the following sub-sections are included in the section related to 'Design of the study':

Participants
Overall procedure
Procedures for data collection and analysis

Participants

This section has a description of the population selected for the study. Population varies in terms of size and specific characteristics. A case study might involve a single person or a group of people. In the case of an experimental study, the researcher would need to use and compare groups, in some cases using existing language classes, in other cases by constructing new groups. This section contains important information about the participants: how the population was selected; the size of the population; the age and other specific characteristics of the population (e.g. academic background, gender, language proficiency level, etc.). In Figure 2.6 (adapted from Benati, Lee, and Hikima 2010: 150) an example of how participants' information is provided in an experimental study is shown.

> The subject pool consisted of 32 participants. They were all English native speakers and they were learning Japanese as part of their second-year undergraduate degree at Cardiff University. To select the population, the following set of criteria were used in this study:
>
> 1. All participants had to be English native speakers.
> 2. They all had to be intermediate-level learners of Japanese.
> 3. They should not have been taught or should not have been previously exposed to the target linguistic feature under investigation.

Figure 2.6 Description of participants in an experimental study

Shoko was a 19-year-old college student in Japan. Being interested in communicating in English, she took and passed the entrance examination to a private women's college specializing in English education, and was placed in the upper-intermediate level according to the placement test the college administered at the beginning of the school year. Shoko was an active and motivated English learner. While in high school, she found communicating in English fascinating and attended a private English conversation school for a year. She spent two weeks home-staying in Canada during the summer vacation between the first and second semesters of her first college year. She also had a Canadian boyfriend during the period the research was conducted. She liked watching English movies and TV shows.

Figure 2.7 Description of participants in a case study

In Figure 2.7 another example, this time in a case study, illustrates how population is described (adapted from Nabei and Swain 2002: 47–48).

Overall Procedure

This is the section where the writer describes in detail the overall design used in the study. In the case of an experimental study, researchers often use a pre- and post-test design with experimental and control groups. Often the researcher is not personally collecting the data to ensure research validity. A brief example is provided in Figure 2.8 (adapted from Benati, Lee, and Hikima 2010: 151–152).

In the second example (see Figure 2.9), the overall procedure used in a case study is described (adapted from Nabei and Swain 2002: 48–49).

The overall procedure section normally includes a brief description of the design (experimental vs case study, for instance), the overall timescale, the main factors or variables under investigations, the role that the researcher played, and an overall description of the analysis adopted (qualitative vs quantitative, for instance).

Procedures for Data Collection and Analysis

The purpose of this section is to describe materials used in the study and explain their functions. Materials include instructional materials and data

> The main purpose of this study was to determine whether positive effects for processing instruction on the Japanese passive form could be found and to measure those effects on sentence-level interpretation and production tasks as well as on discourse-level interpretation tasks. The independent factor in this experiment was the treatment factor, a processing instruction group compared and contrasted to a control group. The dependent factors were the learners' scores on the four tests developed for this study. A pre- and post-test procedure was adopted for this classroom experiment. The pre-tests were administered two days prior to the beginning of the instructional treatment period. All participants were asked to take first the sentence-level interpretation test followed by the sentence-level production test. Participants were then given a very short break lasting only a few moments. The participants then received the two discourse-level interpretation tests. They first heard the story and performed a guided recall. They then listened to a dialogue and performed a guided recall. After the pre-test was administered, the participants were randomly assigned to one of two groups: processing instruction (n = 7) or control group (n = 3). The processing instruction group received two hours of instruction by an instructor who was the researcher and not the subject's regular classroom instructor. The instructor acted as a facilitator for the instructional group as he diligently followed the instructional materials to the letter. The two hours of class time were spent on explanation and practice of the target and also on taking the four post-tests. All the pre-tests and the post-tests were comparable in terms of difficulty and vocabulary. One-way ANOVAs were conducted on the raw scores for all pre-tests to assess whether there were any statistical differences between the two groups before the beginning of the experimental period. Repeated-measures ANOVAs were used on pre-test and post-test scores to assess whether there were any effects for instruction and time.

Figure 2.8 Overall procedure used in an experimental study

collection instruments such as questionnaires, tests, observation schemes, interviews, etc. Equipment used in the study might also be described. The data collection instruments are described in detail, including how they were prepared and what the scoring method was. In Figure 2.10 the

The research involved cycles of a set procedure. A basic cycle was composed of (1) classroom observation and videotaping of a 70-minute class period, (2) administration of a Grammaticality Judgment (GJ) test (Test 1) within a week of the videotaping, followed by (3) a stimulated recall interview with Shoko. This cycle was conducted approximately each week and was repeated six times from the third to eighth week within the 10-week term. In addition, a GJ test (Test 2) composed of all the previously given GJ tests was administered after the term was completed (approximately three weeks after the last cycle). During the classroom observation, one of the researchers was in the back of the room and a video camera was set to capture Shoko and her group members' dialogues and activities. A multi-direction microphone was also set up at the centre of the group table. The taped dialogue was transcribed and analyzed for recast episodes (RE) ...

As noted above, within a week after her group was videotaped, Shoko met with the researcher for approximately one hour outside of class in order to complete the test and to be interviewed. A tailor-made, group-specific GJ test was constructed based on the REs identified earlier during the classroom observation and the videos of her group discussion. After completing the test, a stimulated recall interview based on the videotape was conducted. Scenes of classroom and group activities involving recasts were shown and Shoko was asked to recall and tell what she was thinking at that moment. The baseline question was "What were you thinking then?" A few episodes of other types of feedback and other activity moments were also shown as distracters. The interviews were conducted in Japanese since the information Shoko was asked to deliver was complex. Shoko's verbal reports were audiotaped and later transcribed for analyses.

Figure 2.9 Overall procedure used in a case study

instructional materials and the data collection instruments of an experimental study are briefly described (adapted from Benati, Lee, and Hikima, 2010: 154–165).

In Figure 2.11 another example from a case study is provided (adapted from Nabei and Swain 2002: 50–51).

We developed one packet of instructional materials for the Japanese passive structure. It followed the characteristics of the processing instruction approach to grammar teaching ... Our processing instruction materials consisted of explicit information of the grammatical target structure and information on processing strategies. The explicit information was followed by structured input activities. For this research we developed eight structured input activities; through these activities learners came to interpret the meaning of the grammatical structure in the input. Learners received only limited feedback during instruction ... The L2 learners who formed the control group received no instructional treatment on the targeted feature during the course of the experiment. They were provided a comparable amount of exposure to the target feature in their classroom for the same amount of time. In order to evaluate the effectiveness of the processing instruction treatment on the acquisition of Japanese passive structure and to address the four research questions guiding this study, we developed four different tests. We created two sentence-level assessments, one focused on interpretation and the other production. We created two discourse-level assessments. One presented the discourse as a dialogue and the other presented it as a story. We created two versions of each of the four tests. We used one version as the pre-test and the other as the post-test. We did not simply use one version of each test because pre-testing occurred only two days prior to the treatment and post-testing. We took care to create equivalent versions of the assessments. The pre-tests and post-tests were equal in terms of length, the use of high-frequency vocabulary, and overall difficulty ... One of the sentence-level interpretation tests was an aural task which was developed to measure knowledge gained by learners at interpreting passive forms in Japanese. This test consisted of 20 audiotaped sentences that were recorded by a native-speaker of Japanese speaking at a normal speed. Of the 20 items, 10 were actual targets and the other 10 distracters. The verbs used in these sentences were mostly regular and belonging to two different verb groups. The participants were required to listen to each sentence and to select one of two pictures that matched their interpretation. The two pictures differed in terms of who was performing the action. For the assessment task, learners also had the option of indicating that they were not sure who performed the action. In order to measure real-time comprehension, we did not repeat the items. Learners had only one opportunity to hear and interpret a sentence. Correct responses were given a score of 1 and each incorrect response a score of 0. The maximum score on this test was 10 points and the minimum 0. Distracters were not scored.

Figure 2.10 Procedures for data collection and analysis in an experimental study

The data consisted of REs identified in the classroom discourse, Shoko's verbal reports from the stimulated recall interviews, and GJ test results. A recast in this study was operationally defined as either an isolated or expanded rephrasing of learners' non-target-like utterances provided by the teacher immediately after the non-target-like utterances ... A recast episode (RE) was defined as a sequence of one or more feedback turns, involving at least one recast, to deal with one aspect of non-target-like language use found in a learner's utterance ...

Shoko's interview comments were transcribed and analyzed in the original languages: primarily in Japanese with occasional code mixing of English. A detailed coding scheme was developed based on different facets and levels of awareness in L2 learning. The detailed codes were later selectively categorized under three types of awareness: attention to meaning, attention to language and noticing feedback ... The first author coded the entire interview transcripts and a second coder coded 20% of the data. The inter-coder reliability was 89%. After the coding, the codes were tagged according to each RE. Some REs elicited only 'attention to meaning', whereas others elicited all three.

The total number of items administered in each Grammaticality Judgment test was 76. Test 1 included six weekly short tests; Test 2 was a delayed test composed of the same items. For actual analysis, however, we focused only on 27 items (derived from 14 REs). This was because some items were from ETEs without recasts and others were from REs which were not shown in the stimulated recall sessions due to time constraints. All 14 REs except two contributed a set of two test items: one grammatical and one ungrammatical.

In analyses, Shoko's correct judgment, which is either absolutely or probably correct choices on grammatical sentence items and either absolutely or probably incorrect choices on ungrammatical sentence items, was counted for both Test 1 and 2.

Figure 2.11 Procedures for data collection and analysis in a case study

2.1.5 Results

At this stage in the research paper, the reader is aware of what procedures the researcher used to collect and analyze data. In the results section, the researcher reports on the main findings of the study, providing a summary of what has been found. If an experimental design has been

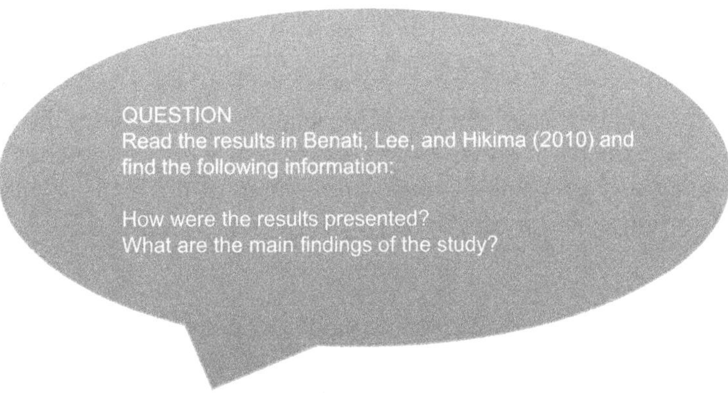

Figure 2.12 Question

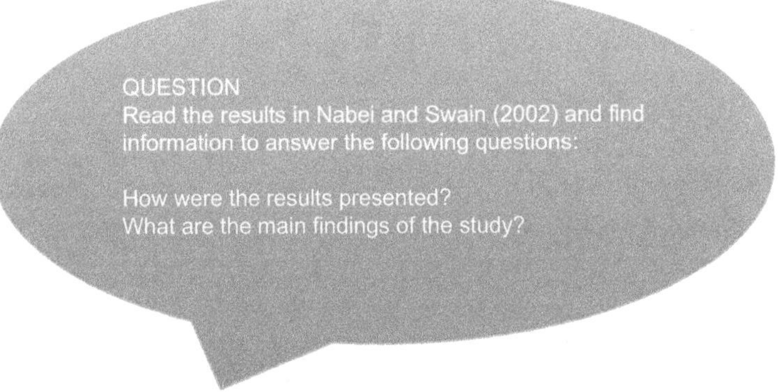

Figure 2.13 Question

used, the researcher will report the average of the scores achieved by each group (mean) and a calculation of the distance between each individual score and the average score (standard deviation). The so-called descriptive statistics (mean and standard deviation) are often presented graphically. Potential differences between and within groups are also reported through statistical analysis (*t*-test, *ANOVA*) where a *p*-value will indicate significance.

Quite often in a case study, both quantitative (e.g. how frequent a behaviour occurred) and qualitative data (e.g. analysis of transcripts from an interview) are presented and analyzed in the result section.

2.1.6 Discussion and Conclusion

In the final part of the research paper, the researcher provides a summary statement of the research results obtained and discusses the meaning of the research findings in relation to the previous literature. The researcher also provides an analysis/reflection of the main results in a broader context and perspective. The final part includes the following sections:

- analysis of the contribution and significance of the results to the general area of research;
- the theoretical, methodological, practical and pedagogical implications of the results obtained;
- recommendations made by the researcher;
- limitations of study undertaken (e.g. small size, lack of delayed post-tests, etc.); and
- suggestions for further research.

2.1.7 References and Appendices

The bibliography section contains the sources and references used and consulted in the study. A reference is a device which locates

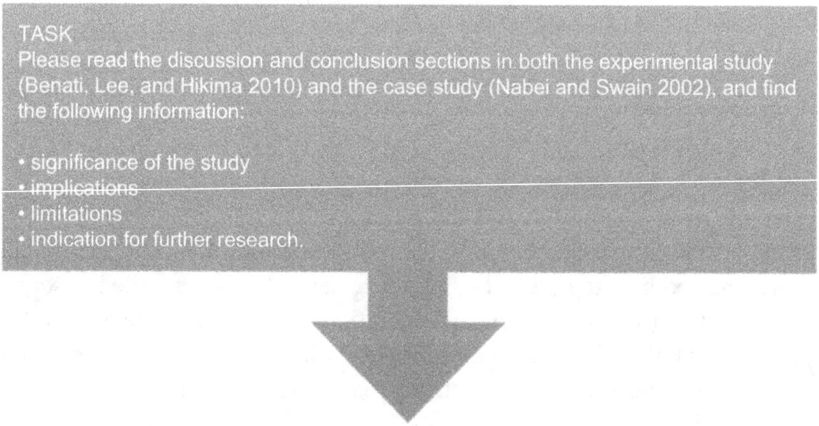

TASK

Please read the discussion and conclusion sections in both the experimental study (Benati, Lee, and Hikima 2010) and the case study (Nabei and Swain 2002), and find the following information:

- significance of the study
- implications
- limitations
- indication for further research.

Figure 2.14 Task

(e.g. books, journal articles, chapters, etc.) anything that has been said or mentioned in the research paper. This section is very important not only because it holds all the citations or the research paper, but also because it provides a database of sources for future research projects. References are normally placed at the end of the research paper using a specific format. The most common format used in journal articles is the APA style (American Psychological Association, 2010). Following this style, a single-author article published in a journal would be as follows:

- author's last name followed by the initials;
- year of publication;
- title of the article;
- name of the journal in italics;
- volume number in italics;
- issue number in parentheses;
- page numbers.

For example:

> Benati, A. (2001). A comparative study of the effects of processing instruction and output-based instruction on the acquisition of the Italian future tense. *Language Teaching Research, 5*(2), 95–127.

Appendices include additional material used during the study such as tests, raw data, interviews, questionnaires or any other procedures used which is too detailed to be included in the main body of the research paper.

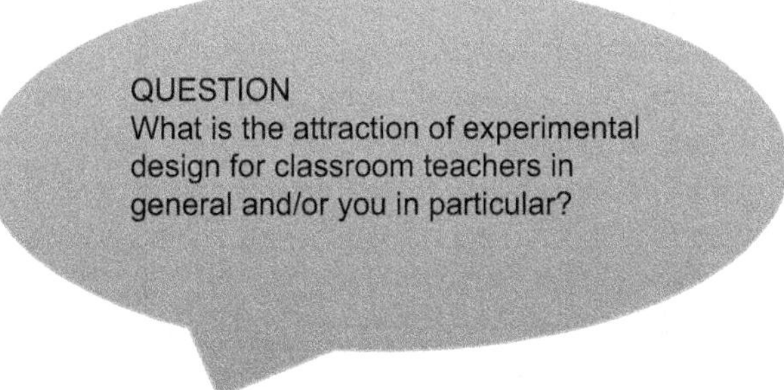

Figure 2.15 Question

2.2 What Is Validity and Reliability?

The main purpose of any scientific research is to make the research design as effective, reliable and valid as possible. The main goal for the researcher is to make sure that the main findings of the study he/she has conducted are valid and reliable both internally and externally. What does this mean? With validity we refer to internal and external validity. Internal invalidity of findings occurs when the findings might have been affected by other factors such as the population selected in the study. External validity is when the results cannot be extended or applied to other contexts and/or the same issues cannot be looked at from a different perspective. Reliability refers to whether the data collection procedures are consistent and accurate. Both validity and reliability will be examined in relation to each of the research frameworks presented in this book and the procedures for collecting data (e.g. questionnaires, tests, interviews, etc.). In this section, some key validity issues are briefly presented.

Validity

One of the main internal factors which has an effect on the internal validity of a study and that might invalidate research findings is the size and the characteristics of participants. The characteristics and number of the subjects taking part in a research project are two important factors that need to be taken into consideration. This is because the researcher must ensure that the population involved in a research project is representative of the general population to which the research applies. This is relevant if we consider that an individual can be affected by a number of individual differences such as attitude, motivation, gender, age, etc. The researcher must ensure that the sample is a representative sample and differences are taken into consideration during the study (e.g. learning experience, proficiency level, language background, etc.). In addition, a small size could magnify the effects of individual variability, and therefore the greater the size, the smaller the effect of individual differences.

Another crucial factor is the calculation of the time needed for data collection. How can the researcher establish how much time is needed to show an effect for a treatment? There is no hard and fast rule for deciding when enough time has been given to collecting a valid sample of data; it is relative to factors such as context, amount of available time, sensitivity of the instruments used to elicit data, etc.

History and maturation are internal validity issues. History refers to the occurrence of any event that is not part of the experimental treatment but which may affect performance on the dependent variable. Maturation is about the physical or mental changes that may occur within the subjects over a period of time. These changes may affect the subjects' performance on the measure of the dependent variable.

The instruments used to collect data could also influence internal validity. Sometimes instruments (task sensitivity) are used as a tool to obtain information about the status of the subject (pre-test used before the experiment). However, the pre-test could affect the internal validity of the experiment, as learners can become test-wise and this practice might affect the subjects' performance. In order to make a study internally valid the researcher needs to be able to demonstrate that the relationship between the independent and dependent variables is unambiguous and not explained by other variables.

Another element of validity to consider is the location for the data collection. The researcher would need to make sure that the environment where the experiment is conducted/data are collected is the same for groups or population.

External validity is concerned with applying and generalizing the findings to situations outside those in which the research was conducted. One of the main factors affecting external validity is again the characteristic of the population. The questions to be addressed are: Can the findings obtained in a study be applied to a different population? Can the effects of an instructional treatment on school-age learners be generalized to adults?

The interaction of subject selection and research is another external factor that might influence the findings of a classroom-based study. Very often volunteers have to be used to collect data. The question which needs to be addressed is: To what degree do paid or volunteer subjects represent the general population to which the research will be generalized? It could be said for instance that volunteers might have a better attitude towards an experiment than existing subjects participating in an experiment. The descriptive explicitness of the independent variable is also a very important factor to be controlled by the researcher. It is crucial to be able to describe the instructional treatment (independent variable) as explicitly as possible, providing details of the way the treatment is implemented. Linked to this latter factor is the possible effect of the research environment. Learners' awareness of taking part in an experiment might affect the behaviour of the sample, the researcher or the experimenter effects: the researcher could have a biased attitude for one method or another.

TASK

Read the following article: VanPatten, B., Borst, S., Collopy, E., Qualin, A., & Price, J. (2013). Explicit information, grammatical sensitivity, and the first-noun strategy: A cross-linguistic study in processing instruction. *The Modern Language Journal* 97(2), 506–527.

Answer the following questions:

a. What do you find in the article that tells you the design was truly experimental or quasi-experimental?

b. Where did the research take place, and who were the students?

c. Can you identify the dependent and independent variables?

d. What are the main findings? Has this study provided an answer to the questions raised?

Procedures

Materials

Assessment instruments and scoring procedure

Main findings

a) Benati, A. (2005). The effects of processing instruction, traditional instruction and meaning–output instruction on the acquisition of English simple past tense. *Language Teaching Research, 9*(1), 67–93.

b) Toth, P. (2006). Processing instruction and a role for output in second language acquisition. *Language Learning, 56*(2), 319–385.

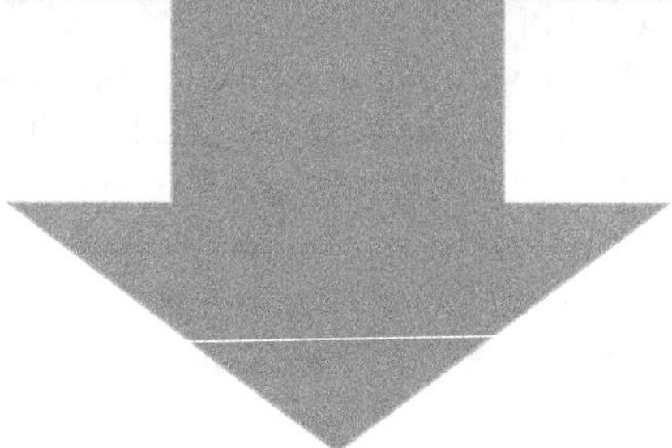

Figure 2.16 Task

Reliability

Reliability also refers to consistency, particularly instrument consistency. It is crucial that the researcher ensures that the tests measure what they are supposed to measure. Also the researchers need to establish the interval between test administration (pre- and post-tests) and whether participants can become test-wise. The main concept is that for an instrument to be reliable it must demonstrate that if a participant takes a test and receives a low score, it would be expected that if the same participant took the test again they would receive a low score again.

These and other reliability and validity issues will be discussed in Part Two of this book in relation to individual methodological second language research frameworks.

2.3 What Are the Key Terms?

Literature review is conducted to carefully examine and evaluate research and theory related to an area of enquiry. As with any analysis, this requires breaking the subject down into its component parts. Examining these components helps the researcher to identify gaps in the knowledge and formulate specific research questions.

Reliability is addressing the main question as to whether an independent researcher carrying out the same study would obtain the same results. Reliability refers to the extent to which the findings from one study can be generalized to a different context, population and perspective.

Validity is addressing the main questions as to whether what has been measured in a study is what was supposed to be measured. Both internal and external validity must be considered.

2.4 What Are the Key Readings?

American Psychological Association. (2010). *Publication Manual of the American Psychological Association*. Washington, DC: American Psychological Association.

Benati, A. (2005). The effects of processing instruction, traditional instruction and meaning–output instruction on the acquisition of English simple past tense. *Language Teaching Research*, *9*(1), 67–93. http://dx.doi.org/10.1191/1362168805lr154oa

Benati, A., Lee, J., & Hikima, N. (2010). Exploring the effects of processing instruction on discourse-level interpretation tasks with the Japanese passive construction. In A. Benati & J. Lee. *Processing Instruction and Discourse*, (pp. 148–177). London: Continuum.

Hollyday, A. (2007). *Doing and Writing Qualitative Research*. London: SAGE.

Nabei, T., & Swain, M. (2002). Learner awareness of recasts in classroom interaction: A case study of an adult EFL student's second language learning. *Language Awareness*, *11*(1), 43–63. http://dx.doi.org/10.1080/09658410208667045

Oliver, R. (1995). Negative Feedback in Child NS-NNS Conversation. *Studies in Second Language Acquisition, 17,* 459–481.

Paltridge, B., & Phakti, A. (Eds.). (2010). *Continuum Companion to Research Methods in Applied Linguistics*. London: Continuum.

Toth, P. (2006). Processing instruction and a role for output in second language acquisition. *Language Learning*, *56*(2), 319–385. http://dx.doi.org/10.1111/j.0023-8333.2006.00349.x

Part Two
Key Methodological Frameworks

This section of the book is written to introduce novice readers to the basic concepts and components of each of the methodological research frameworks presented, and makes use of a number of exemplary studies to illustrate the key phases of the various designs, grouped into four main methodological frameworks (Action Research in Chapter 3, Experimental in Chapter 4, Observation in Chapter 5, and Case Study in Chapter 6).

To accomplish this, each chapter will contain the following features:

Key Concepts and Components
Key Data Collection and Analysis Procedures
Key Advantages and Disadvantages
Key Exemplary Study
Key Terms
Key Readings

3 Action Research Framework

Chapter Preview

In this chapter the main components of the action research approach to second language research and the considerations and steps involved in implementing an action research will be presented and analyzed. The advantages and threats of using this framework will be explored. An exemplary study will be presented to show and to describe to readers how action research is conducted and how findings are presented. Sources for further reading will be provided.

3.1 What Are the Key Concepts and Components?

Action research is a very effective research approach to undertake a small-scale investigation by a teacher in the language classroom. Through action research, teachers can engage in research related to specific language problems in order to improve materials, language teaching methodologies and curriculum development. They can also undertake research for their own professional development.

Action research is often motivated by teachers reflecting on their own current teaching. An action researcher may undertake a project individually in the classroom, or co-operate with colleagues in investigating a question or a problem. LoCastro (1994: 5) has defined action research as "... one form of classroom-centred research which is seen as being small scale and situational ... focused on a particular problem, to try to understand and perhaps solve some concrete problem in an individual teacher's classroom." Action research can be defined as a process designed to address more effective ways in teaching languages and facilitating learning through identifying a specific problem, targeting the causes of the problem through systematic data collection procedures (e.g. surveys, observation, interviews) and applying an effective solution to the problem as a result of the data being collected and interpreted.

Ellis (1997: 200) has identified three main motivational factors used by teachers to develop an initial research question:

- theory and previously published research;
- replication of previous research;
- micro-evaluations of courses, programmes or materials.

If teachers are kept up to date with theory and research findings in language learning, not only they would improve their pedagogical practices, but also they would find the stimulus to conduct their own research to micro-evaluate teaching materials, or particular teaching and learning problems arising in their own classroom. Markee (1996) identifies six characteristics in the action research framework:

1. it is carried out by insiders;
2. it uses both qualitative or quantitative data;
3. it is for the purpose of teacher behavioural and attitudinal change;
4. it has no expectation of generalizability;
5. it seeks to improve classroom practice; and
6. it aims at the development of a teacher theory.

The fundamental elements of action research are the following:

- Action research analyzes the human actions and social situations that students and teachers experience.
- Action research uses an exploratory approach; it aims to explain what happens in the classroom in relation to specific teaching contents.
- Action research interprets the different classroom events from the point of view of those who take part in each situation; that is, it involves teachers and students: their beliefs, values, intentions, decisions.
- Action research uses very direct and simple language to explain the classroom situations that are analyzed, far from the technical and specialized language used by conventional research.

Nunan (1989) defines action research as a research framework composed of the following stages:

1. identifying a 'problem';
2. describing the 'problem';

3. planning the research;
4. intervening;
5. evaluating the results;
6. writing a report and disseminating results;
7. following up.

At the beginning the teacher identifies an issue or a 'problem' concerning an aspect of language learning in a classroom context (Stage 1). The 'problem' is often something that is noticeable and persistent. The teacher decides to evaluate the extent of the 'problem' through reflection, observation and discussion with the students and other colleagues (baseline data). Let's assume that the problem the teacher has identified is that students in the classroom always find it difficult to learn a specific grammatical feature of the language they are currently learning. The teacher finds and reads relevant texts that provide him/her with a better understanding of the specific problem. He/she hopes that research could somehow help him/her to find some solutions to the problem. The next step is to describe the 'problem' and to find out whether it is a common issue (Stage 2). The teacher spends time observing the class and taking notes of his/her students' behaviour. After observation, the teacher forms a question or hypothesis as to the cause of the problem. He/she reaches this stage by reading and reflecting on literature (articles, surveys, reports) which has described similar problems. The cause of the 'problem' might be that students need better practice and need to be exposed to more effective materials to master the grammatical feature.

At this stage (Stage 3) the teacher decides to engage in some form of systematic investigation to solve the problem. He/she creates an action research plan (Stage 4) which includes the following:

- a specific purpose;
- actionable research questions;
- ideas for data collection and analysis;
- a timeline; and
- an evaluation plan.

To this end, he/she produces some new material to teach the students the target grammatical form. The teacher implements the new pedagogical approach in the classroom in an attempt to solve the problem. After a few weeks, the teacher observes a higher level of performance among his/her students, where previously most of the students were making mistakes and not responding well to the material used. Several of the students now have improved accuracy and fluency in using the particular target form. The teacher sees a dramatic turnaround in students' ability to use the form correctly and appropriately, and he/she concludes that this is in part due to the data gathered through action research. The teacher is now ready to share the findings with others (Stage 6). The teacher has noticed that students understand better and perform much better than before. He/she then decides to disseminate and share his/her findings with other teachers. Teachers can share the findings of their action research projects in local teachers' meetings as a presentation, in informal meetings with other colleagues, or by publishing their results for a larger body of readers. Action research reports get read, and appear to have greater immediate impact on the lives and practices of other classroom teachers than the findings of second language researchers.

The teacher looks now for other methods to solve his/her original classroom problem (Stage 7). The teacher makes some recommendations and suggests that the new approach used (the one used in the data collection) is a very effective way to learn and teach the grammatical feature. The follow-up of the action research is to show other teachers that the dynamics/problems present in a particular context might also be present in their contexts. This will hopefully spur other teachers on to starting action research projects of their own.

The action research framework could be a very effective approach to research in addressing a practical problem and providing a practical pedagogical solution. This research framework is initiated by a 'problem' the teacher has noticed (awareness and reflection phase) in students learning a language. Subsequently, the teacher decides to take action (research plan and implementation phase) and a different instructional intervention is devised. At the end the teacher conducts an evaluation of the intervention and disseminates the results to the public (evaluation and dissemination phase). Hopefully, the findings from this research would have an impact in improving students' learning experience and language teaching.

The advantages of using action research are clear. Apart from improving teachers' language methodology, teachers will gain a greater insight into what is going on in the minds of their students. Action research also improves communication between teacher and student, and networks with other educators. Teachers can become very proactive through action research and develop a clear idea of what should be done in the language classroom.

Ellis (1997) has assigned four main roles to action research: exploratory; emancipatory; useful for curriculum development; and useful for developing teacher awareness. It provides an insight into language learning

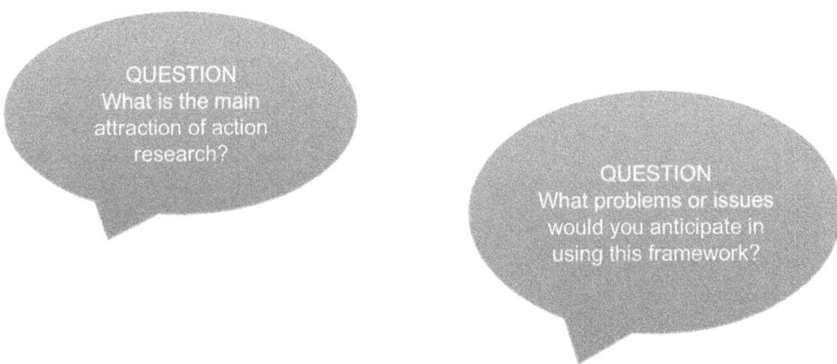

Figure 3.1 Question

processes. Teachers can also evaluate their teaching. There is a great deal teachers can learn about the way they teach through simple observations. Action research can help teachers to incorporate principled change into their teaching. A number of different data collection tools can be used within this framework: progress tests, field notes, diaries, questionnaires, interviews, introspection and observation.

3.2 What Are the Key Data Collection and Analysis Procedures?

There are no hard and fast rules about how to collect and analyze data in an action research framework. Figure 3.2 shows the continuous nature of the process. Action research never really ends because learning is a cyclical process. The researcher is involved in observing, designing, assessing and reporting during the entire process. Initially, the action researcher would notice and become aware of a problem, a situation or an issue. This first consideration is followed by a period of exploration and reflection where the researcher might engage in a number of steps: identify the problem and evaluate some of the possible reasons and causes; engage in an initial observation (baseline data) and keep a diary to jot down what is happening; brainstorm possible solutions to the problem; initiate a literature review where the action researcher is trying to find out if others have dealt with the same problem and what they have found. The third phase is the creation of a plan. Before engaging in the research, the action researcher plans a kind of backbone for the study, a skeletal frame on which

Figure 3.2 Action Research methodological framework

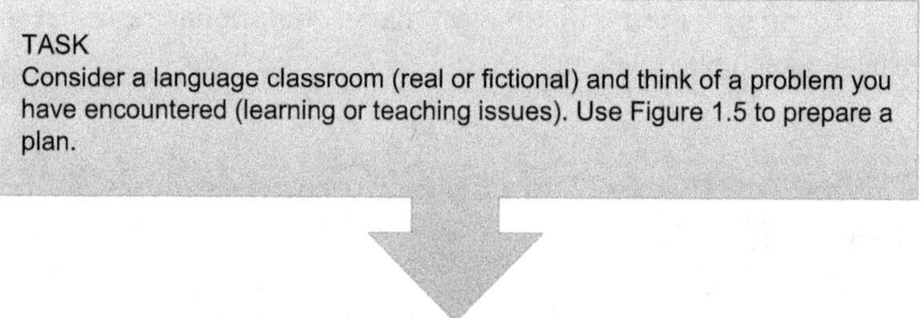

Figure 3.3 Task

to base the actions and timeline. In creating the plan the researcher needs to develop a hypothesis/research question and continue reviewing the relevant literature so that he/she can develop an idea of the kind of data that needs to be collected. The next step is to implement the action research plan. Data are usually gathered from many sources of information over a period of time. This provides a broader and deeper understanding of students' knowledge and learning. Among the different classroom data collection tools available for action research are: observations (checklists, notes, etc.), interviews and conversations, student work, grades and tests.

The final step in action research is evaluating and reporting the results. After planning, teaching and collecting the data, it is very important to evaluate the results of the action research and make instructional decisions

Information about the respondent

Name:

Age (please circle): 18–24 25–39 40–54 55+

Gender (please circle): Male Female

Is English your first language? (please circle): YES NO

What is your profession?

Figure 3.4 Factual data in surveys

Attitudinal Data are: Attitudes – Beliefs – Opinions – Values – Interests

EX: The teacher's ability to teach grammar were (please circle)

High

Average

Low

Behavioural Data are: Actions – Lifestyles – History – Experience

EX: What kind of approach does the teacher use to explain and practice grammar?

Figure 3.5 Behavioural and attitudinal data in surveys

based on the findings. The results will indicate to the action researcher whether to continue with current practices or revise them. Reporting entails finding a way for the researcher to disseminate the findings. This is a process that usually includes the following: presenting the findings to a colleague or to a professional forum (e.g. meeting); submitting a proposal to a conference; writing up the action research; and deciding on the next step to take.

One specific data collection instrument used in action research is a survey. Nunan and Bailey (2009: 125) define a survey as "a snapshot of conditions, attitudes, and/or events of an entire population at a single point in time by collecting data from a sample drawn from the population." The type of data collected in a survey will depend on the purpose of the study. Surveys can be used to collect descriptive and factual data (see Figure 3.4) or behavioural and attitudinal data (see Figure 3.5). 'Factual data' refers

TASK
You are planning to conduct a survey. Decide on the following:
- construct;
- population;
- sample selection and size;
- data collection instrument.

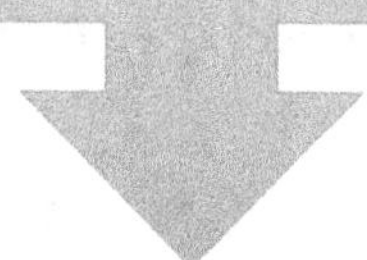

Figure 3.6 Task

to information about the participants – information such as age, gender, place of birth, education, ethnicity, etc. 'Behavioural data' refers to actions that participants do. 'Attitudinal data' involves capturing what the respondents think. In order to develop a survey we need to consider the following issues:

- identifying the construct to be investigated;
- deciding on the population; and
- selecting the sample and deciding the number to be surveyed.

The first step in using a survey is to identify and define the construct and the purpose of the research. Once this has been established the researcher needs to decide the focus of analysis of the survey, which could be students, teachers, practitioners, language assistants, language departments, etc. A final step is to select a sample and number of the respondents to be surveyed. The sample will determine the level of generalization that can be claimed. There are different types of sampling technique which can be used and this very much depends on the purpose of the survey. Researchers can use existing samples of population (convenience sample), random samples by pulling names out of a hat, stratified samples from random samples of homogeneous subgroups (males and females for example), and purposeful samples where specific knowledgeable groups are selected for the survey.

Surveys in second language research can be useful in providing information about curriculum development, programme evaluation and the research of certain topics.

3.3 What Are the Key Advantages and Disadvantages?

The action research framework is used for teachers to address practical issues in the language classroom and collect their own data. This research framework has a number of benefits. First, it is very effective in encouraging teachers to reflect on their own practices. This in turn can lead to changes and improvements in language pedagogy. Second, it provides teachers with opportunities to enrich their theoretical knowledge on a particular issue related to language learning. Third, it allows teachers to develop the skill of conducting their own research in the classroom and contributing to the current debate in second language learning and teaching.

Despite the fact that there are clearly important advantages in adopting action research as a research framework, there are also some methodological disadvantages that the potential researcher/teacher needs to be aware of. Nunan (1990: 64) has argued that action research "lacks the rigor of true scientific research". The design might be less systematic and more informal than the experimental research framework. Teachers are not in the position to be absolutely sure that students' performance is in any way related to the administration of the new material (treatment), for instance. It could be argued that improvement in performance is caused by other variables the teacher did not control (e.g. previous knowledge, fatigue, individual differences, etc.). In the absence of a pre-test, the teacher does not have any measurement of student's knowledge before the beginning of the instructional treatment. With the lack of a control group, there is no measure of the relative effects of the instructional treatment vs no treatment. In addition to that, the teacher is not in a position to say whether the performance is due to a particular component of the treatment (explicit information or a particular task), as we do not have a specific and detailed description of the treatment. In general terms, findings based on action research have to be very careful about generalizability because other uncontrolled factors may be involved.

Another possible threat in using action research is the formulation of researchable questions. Teachers have ideas and intuitions about classroom learning problems, but this is quite different from developing and formulating a researchable question. A researchable question is one that should be formulated through a critical review of the existing and relevant literature and can be answered through research. This is not often the case for action research.

An additional problem area is how findings are reported. The findings from action research are not normally disseminated through a written report or a journal article. Very often they are briefings, verbal reports, meetings or presentations at a local level and within the institution and organization where the research took place. Because of its scope and dissemination goals, action research does not need to conform to the objectives and the methods of experimental research. It is less necessary to establish reliability and validity or methods and procedures.

Despite the fact that action research addresses real-life problems and promotes changes, there are some possible barriers in starting an action research project. First of all, there is the difficulty around the development of a clear research idea. Most projects within this framework begin with a simple idea which might be noticing something or wondering why something is the case. Problems are the key stimuli for action research projects. After identifying a particular problem, teachers write their research idea as a question with the intent of finding a solution for the problem. For example, "Why do my students show very low levels of motivation and participation in class?" is still a vague, general question to answer, but teachers might be able to address the question and provide an answer through systematic observation, surveys or another research instrument. Teachers' teaching and understanding of the processes involved in learning acquisition are enhanced by the insights gained in the literature search.

3.4 What Does an Action Research Study Look Like?

In this section a typical action research study is presented (Sampson 2012). The intent is to show readers how action research is carried out in the language classroom and describe the different components of this research framework. The title of the study is: "The language-learning self, self-enhancement activities, and self-perceptual change".

Purpose of the Study

In this exemplary study (description of the study adapted from Sampson 2012), the researcher's main purpose was to conduct action research in an English as a Foreign Language context in the attempt to explore factors related to motivation among university-level students. More specifically, the study investigated the possible relationship between individual self-images, socially constructed self-images and language learning motivation. The study is theoretically grounded on the analysis of Dörnyei (2009)'s three elements in the L2 Motivational Self System framework (see description in the next section). In addition, the author identifies the need for qualitative and quantitative research in Japanese L2 motivation research and the importance of using a variety of data collection tools (triangulation) to strengthen methodology.

Research Questions

The main idea behind this action research study evolved from an observation by the teacher-researcher of a lack of focus in the way learners studied English. The teacher-researcher applied ideas from Dörnyei's (2009) second language motivational self-system to provide more focus to the learning endeavours of his students. Dorneyei's model is composed of three elements: the Ideal L2 Self (the image of who we wish to become); the Ought-to L2 Self (the attributes we ought to possess to be successful); and motives generated in the learning environment (teacher, curriculum, lesson style). Three research questions (Sampson 2012: 320) emerged during three cycles of action research conducted over the course of one semester of study (15 weeks):

1. If information is collected about students' vision of their future English self, in what way will this facilitate the development of more motivating lessons? (Cycle 1)
2. If activities proposed as building a possible self-conception are integrated into lessons, what elements might students perceive as motivating? (Cycles 2, 3)
3. If activities proposed as building a possible self-conception are integrated into lessons, in what way will students perceive a change to their L2 self-image? (Cycles 2, 3)

Method

Participants

Thirty-four students in three different classes participated in the study. They were all Japanese native speakers (all females) and were learning English (first year of study) in a Japanese university. They were all first year students studying in the Faculty of International Communication. Their level of English was mixed.

Procedures for Data Collection

Introspective methods were used in this study, particularly with the main purpose of collecting learners' views about learning experiences and their self-images. Different data collection procedures were used over a three-cycle period. In each cycle the teacher-research reflected on the data to enact a change action. In Cycle 1 a free writing activity was used to collect information from students on their ideal life in the future after studying English. Based on the responses a number of tasks enhancing the ideal-self concept were used in Cycle 2. Students were asked to provide feedback on learning and practices during Cycle 2. They were asked to complete a session entry in their learning journal. They were asked to reflect, at the end of each session, on the tasks and learning experience during the class. Based on the data analysis of Cycle 2, a greater emphasis was given to activities focusing on development of ideal-self in Cycle 3. Students were asked to make a conversation skit reflecting on the semester's main tasks. In addition, a learning experience questionnaire was administered to all students at the end of the process. The questionnaire was both quantitative and qualitative in nature (numerical scale with additional open-ended components).

The Enhancement Programme

During the three cycles of action research an enhancement programme of 10 sessions was implemented. The programme include a number of self-enhancement activities (see a representative list below):

- Students wrote ideas about their one-year/15-year future ideal-selves under different life areas.
- Student pairs ranked pictures of different futures in English (jobs, lifestyles, etc.).
- Student groups discussed different high-profile people to select a role-model speaker to come to class.

Results and Interpretation

Research question 1: If information is collected about students' vision of their future English self, in what way will this facilitate the development of more motivating lessons?

The results from the free-writing task clearly indicated that only a few students had a developed vision of their future self. They might have an idea of their future intentions, but the idea of the ideal-self is not detailed. However, a number of general themes of imagined future emerged in the analysis of the free-writing task. Among the main areas identified were living abroad and communicating with people of other countries. The teacher-researcher was able to use these themes in the self-enhancement sessions in the hope of creating a more motivating environment.

Research question 2: If activities proposed as building a possible self-conception are integrated into lessons, what elements might students perceive as motivating?

The analysis of the learning journal entries, the reflective skit and the final questionnaire provided the following findings:

- Activities focusing in steps towards the development of the ideal self were considered highly motivating.
- Activities focusing on the ideal-future self or those that focused on the 'failed' future self were also considered motivating activities by students.
- Activities that included a social component helped motivating students in a number of ways: broadening their thinking; giving a greater sense of possibility; providing support for thinking about one's future self.

Research question 3: If activities proposed as building a possible self-conception are integrated into lessons, in what way will students perceive a change to their L2 self-image?

As a result of the data collected through the initial free-writing task, the teacher-researcher introduced (change action) a number of activities in the enhancement sessions programme that focused on the development of self-images in the hope that this would have some positive effects on building L2 self-ideal conception and motivation. The analysis of the learning journal entries and the final questionnaires revealed the following:

- Students discussed how their self-image had become more detailed.
- Students noticed a gap between the self and their ideal self and therefore they were more motivated to find out their ideal self.
- Students developed a better concept of the importance of self.

These findings showed how students have begun to connect their studies with their self-image.

Conclusion

The main aim of this study was based on the view that helping students to focus on their self-mage in learning might increase motivation and ability to learn. The research was based on a three-cycle approach, with a first cycle of action research revealing that only a few students had a developed vision of their future self. Action was taken in order to create motivating learning sessions and enhance the self-images of learners. The results of this study confirmed that consultation with students about their self-images helped to create motivating lessons that enhanced learners' self-images.

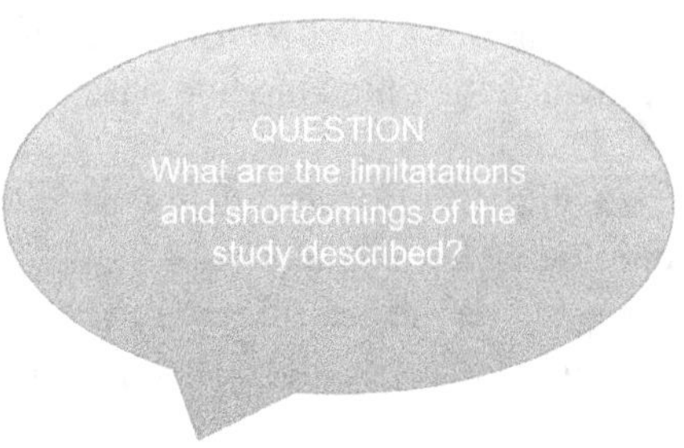

Figure 3.7 Question

TASK

Read this article: Sampson, R. (2012). The language-learning self, self-enhancement activities, and self perceptual change. *Language Teaching Research*, *16*(3): 317–335. Answer the following questions:

1. What is the purpose of the research?
2. What are the research questions?
3. What are the main findings?
4. Are you convinced? Do you have any objections about the research framework?

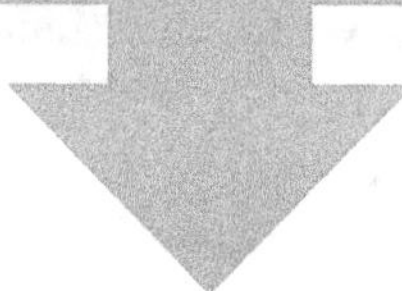

Figure 3.8 Task

3.5 What Are the Key Terms?

Identifying a problem is the initial step in action research. The researcher becomes aware of a problem or an issue in the language classroom concerning teaching or leaning processes.

Describing the problem is the ability of the action researcher to reflect and critically explore what he/she has noticed.

Planning the research is the development of a strategy for improving the situation. The researcher develops a plan of action in order to bring about improvement.

Intervening is the step taken by the action researcher to collect the data and implement the plan.

Evaluating the results involves a reflection on the action of the researcher after collecting and analyzing the data. The evaluation process involves a revision of the process and the instruments used in the action research project.

Writing a report and disseminating results are steps taken by the action researcher to inform the community about the results obtained in the study and its wider implications.

Following up is the step in action research where the researcher might identify additional questions emerging from the data and plan for further plans and steps.

3.6 What Are the Key Readings?

Burns, A. (2005). Action research. In E. Hinkel (Ed.), *Handbook of Research in Second Language Teaching and Learning*, (pp. 241–256). Mahwah, NJ: Lawrence Erlbaum.

Burns, A. (2010). *Doing Action Research in English Language Teaching: A Guide to Practitioners*. New York, NY: Routledge.

Ellis, R. (1997). SLA and language pedagogy: An educational perspective. *Studies in Second Language Acquisition, 19*(01), 69–92. http://dx.doi.org/10.1017/S0272263197001058

Greenwood, D., & Levin, M. (2007). *Introduction to Action Research: Social Research for Social Change* (2nd ed.). Thousand Oaks, CA: SAGE.

LoCastro, V. (1994). Teachers helping themselves: Classroom research and action research. *Language Teaching, 18*, 4–7.

Mackey, A., Gass, S., Dörnyei, Z., & Czizér, K. (2012). *How to Design and Analyze Surveys in Second Language Acquisition Research.* Malden, MA: Wiley–Blackwell.

Markee, N. (1996). Making second language classroom research work. In J. Schachter, & S. Gass (Eds.). *Second Language Classroom Research: Issues and Opportunities*, (pp. 117–155). Mahwah, NJ: Lawrence Erlbaum.

McNiff, J., & Whitehead, J. (2006). *All You Need to Know About Action Research.* Thousand Oaks, CA: SAGE.

Mertler, G. (2006). *Action Research: Teachers as Researchers in the Classroom.* Thousand Oaks, CA: SAGE.

Nunan, D. (2005). Classroom research. In E. Hinkel (Ed.), *Handbook of Research in Second Language Teaching and Learning*, (pp. 225–240). Mahwah, NJ: Lawrence Erlbaum.

Pine, G. (2009). *Teacher Action Research.* Thousand Oaks, CA: SAGE.

Sampson, R. (2012). The language-learning self, self-enhancement activities, and self-perceptual change. *Language Teaching Research, 16*(3), 317–335. http://dx.doi.org/10.1177/1362168812436898

Stringer, E. (2007). *Action Research.* Thousand Oaks, CA: SAGE.

4 Experimental Research Framework

Chapter Preview

In this chapter the basic structure and function of the experimental research framework will be introduced and explained. Key procedures to collect and analyze data within an experimental research framework will be presented. The advantages and disadvantages of using this framework will be explored. An exemplary study will be presented to show and to describe how an experimental study is conducted and how findings are presented. Key terms associated with experimental research and sources for further reading will be provided.

4.1 What Are the Key Concepts and Components?

The experimental research framework is the most common research framework currently used in second language research. One of the essential characteristics of the experimental research framework is that the researcher must systematically control and manipulate a number of variables in order to establish a casual relationship between the so-called independent and dependent factors. Experiments involve manipulation and control of extraneous variables which might be influencing the outcomes of a study. Seliger and Shohamy (1989: 10) argue that experimental research generally consists of at least three components:

1. questions/hypotheses generated from a critical review of previous research and theory;
2. data collection procedures;
3. data analysis procedures to analyze and interpret the data collected.

We can characterize these components as follows:

1. In order to carry out any type of experimental research, a specific research problem needs to be identified, a 'problem' which requires

a solution or further investigation. Questions and hypotheses are generated as a result of critically analyzing existing theoretical views and current empirical research on a specific area of enquiry of second language acquisition.

2. In order to attempt to address research questions or hypotheses formulated on a specific area of enquiry, a number of data collection procedures can be used. Different procedures can be adopted to collect data according to the nature of the experimental study.
3. In order to analyze and interpret the data collected, a number of data analysis procedures can be used. The analysis and interpretation of the data collected will provide an answer to the questions and/or hypotheses raised.

4.1.1 Experimental Designs

Experimental research is carried out to explore the strength of a relationship between variables. Scholars and practitioners are often interested in investigating the effects of factors such as a particular 'teaching approach' on language learners' performance. Learners' performance is usually measured through a test. The 'teaching approach' is given the label of *independent variable*, and it is expected that this variable would influence the other variable (the test), called the *dependent variable.*

Cook and Campbell (1979: 5) offered a clear and overall description of the experimental research framework: "All experiments involve at least a treatment, an outcome measure, units of assignment, and some comparison from which change can be inferred and hopefully attributed to the treatment."

Experimental research is carefully planned and constructed so that the variables involved in the study are controlled and manipulated. From Cook and Campbell's description, three main components can be identified in experimental research framework:

1. participants ('units of assignment');
2. instructional treatment ('treatment' or independent variable);
3. measurement of the instructional treatment ('outcome measure' or dependent variable).

We can expand on these brief designations:

1. The main objective of experimental research is to measure the relative effects of different instructional treatments given to participants

arranged in groups. Comparison is the essence of experimental research. Groups can be formed by the researcher specifically for an experiment or pre-existing groups can be used. In forming experimental groups, the researcher needs to take into account the subject's variability. Randomization or matching procedures are normally used to make sure that individual variables are distributed homogenously across groups. Control is a central concern in experimental studies. Researchers must make any efforts and take actions to control, reduce or possibly eliminate factors except the ones under investigation. For instance, the research might ensure that the groups are taught at the same time of the day to eliminate the 'fatigue' factor, or that the same teacher is instructing the groups, etc.

2. The instructional treatment is the independent variable in an experimental research design and it is specifically constructed for the experiment. An instructional treatment refers to a technique, method or material presented under controlled circumstances. It is the variable that the researcher suspects may influence the dependent variable. A new grammar method might be very effective in improving learners' accuracy in producing a sentence or discourse containing a particular grammatical feature. The researcher chooses independent variables to measure their effects in relation to the dependent variables.
3. The measurement of the instructional treatment is the way in which the effects of the treatment are evaluated and observed. Different types of test are the logical way to evaluate the effectiveness of a treatment. Scores from a data-gathering instrument usually provide information about the effectiveness of the independent variable. The dependent variable is the major and central variable that will be measured in an experimental study. There can be more than one in a study. Participants are usually tested prior to receiving their treatment (pre-test) and after the instructional treatment (post-test) to measure the possible effects of the treatment factor. Experimental research makes use of pre-test/post-test designs.

Within the experimental research framework, the independent factor is therefore a stimulus (e.g. a new method, a new technique) and the dependent factor is a response to that stimulus (e.g. a student's performance on a test). Experiments in classroom settings are usually of two types: quasi-experimental (without random assignment) or truly experimental (with random assignment). The main difference between these two approaches is that in a truly experimental design the researcher undertakes his/her research with groups that have been constituted through the use of a random procedure. Random assignment ensures that participants have an equal chance to be assigned to groups. In quasi-experimental and truly experimental design a comparison is made between two or more groups. There are two types of groups comparison: two or more groups receiving different treatments; two or more groups receiving different treatments, and one of them receiving no treatment (control group).

4.1.2 One-shot Design

The one-shot design is used for pilot studies where researchers want to try out treatments or tests before entering a full experimental design. It is a very basic design and involves the use of a single treatment, a single group and a single post-test.

Example: A researcher develops new materials for teaching Italian gender agreement and wants to investigate its effectiveness. The new material (treatment-independent variable) is administered to a group. At the end of the instructional treatment, the group is tested (measurement of the treatment-dependent variable) in the use of gender agreement in Italian and the researcher finds out that participants have scored well in the test. The researcher concludes that the new material is the causative factor for participants' performance in the test.

One of the main concerns with this type of design is that it does not control for other factors that might have determined the final findings. An important concept in experimental research is control. Control requires the reduction and possible elimination of other factors (apart from the independent variable) which can be considered responsible for learners' performance. The researcher has no information about the individual characteristics of the group involved in the study before the beginning of the experiment. There is no information available about learners' previous knowledge of 'gender agreement' in Italian. The researcher has not used a pre-test/post-test design.

4.1.2 Quasi-experimental Design

This design is also called quasi-experimental and is very economical as it allows the use of existing groups rather than assigning participants to groups through a randomization or matching procedure (see Shadish and Luellen 2006 for a detailed description of quasi-experimental design).

Example: A researcher wants to investigate the effectiveness of a 'new treatment' in the teaching of Japanese passive constructions. A treatment group receiving the 'new treatment' and a control group receiving no treatment are compared at the beginning of the experiment by means of pre-tests, and are later compared at the end of the experimental period by means of post-tests. The statistical analysis reveals that the treatment group scores are higher than the control group scores in the post-tests.

One concern with this design is that we are not sure whether the two groups are equivalent before the treatment. One way to avoid this is to match the participants in the two groups according to various characteristics (sex, aptitude, language, scores, etc.). This would increase the comparability of the groups. Researchers also use randomization procedures to assign participants to groups so that extraneous variables are equally distributed by chance between the groups.

4.1.3 Truly Experimental Design

The difference between this design (see Figure 4.1 for a visual representation) and the quasi-experimental design is that it involves the use of two or more groups which have been formed through a process of randomization. Randomization would ensure that subjects are equally distributed to groups and by doing that it is assumed that all the 'independent variables' are controlled. If groups are made equivalent before the beginning of the instructional period then any other possible extraneous variables might be equally distributed across all groups. Many of the possible validity threats are controlled in this pre-test/post-test design.

Example: A researcher intends to compare the relative effects of two different instructional interventions (independent variable) on the acquisition of English past tense regular forms. Participants are randomly assigned to three groups. The first group receive an innovative instructional treatment and the second group a more traditional instructional treatment. A control group is also used. This group is not exposed to any treatment. Two tests (dependent variable) are developed and consist of an aural interpretation

Figure 4.1 Visual representation of a truly experimental design

task and a written completion production task at sentence level. A pre-test/post-test design is adopted. The scores are measured with the use of statistical analysis procedures which reveal that participants in the innovative group perform better than participants in the traditional group and the control group in all measures.

4.2 What Are the Key Data Collection and Analysis Procedures?

Tests are commonly used as an instrument to collect data about participants' knowledge and performance on a number of areas such as grammar, metalinguistic awareness, vocabulary and overall proficiency. In experimental study, tests (dependent variable) are used to measure the effects of the independent variable (e.g. method, technique, instructional approaches). In this section a sample of three tests developed and used for experimental research will be presented: Interpretation Test; Recall and Multiple Choice Tests; Grammaticality Judgment Test.

4.2.1 Assessment Measures

Interpretation Test

An interpretation test is used to measure the ability of learners to interpret sentences or discourse containing a targeted linguistic feature. The interpretation test in Figure 4.2 (Benati, 2004) was developed to test whether L2 learners are able to process sentences containing Italian gender agreement (masculine vs feminine forms). It consists of 20 audio-taped sentences with 10 of these actual targets (masculine (*-o-*) and feminine endings (*-a*) and the other 10 distracters. Specifically, the distracters were adjectives ending with *-e*. As in the treatment materials, the items on the pre-tests and post-tests described an object or a person represented by two different pictures. The learners' task is to determine which person or object is being described. They could chose between the two pictures or choose the "not sure" option. Care is taken so that the test is balanced in terms of difficulty and vocabulary. Because beginning level learners are examined, high frequency vocabulary items are used. Correct responses are given a score of 1 and each incorrect response receive a score of 0. The maximum possible score is 10 points whereas the minimum possible score was 0 points.

Interpretation test (adjective)
Listen to each sentence in which a person or an object is described and determine which person or object is described. If you are not sure tick the other box!

1.

□	□	□
picture of Bill Clinton	picture of Hilary Clinton	I am not sure

2.

□	□	□
picture of a fat woman	picture of a fat man	I am not sure

3.

□	□	□
picture of a slim man	picture of a slim woman	I am not sure

4.

□	□	□
picture of a famous actor	picture of a famous actress	I am not sure

5.

□	□	□
picture of a famous male singer	picture of a famous female singer	I am not sure

Sentences heard by learners

1. È stupido; 2. È grassa; 3. È magra; 4. È famoso; 5. È bravo (from Benati & Lee, 2008)

(the test continues in a similar fashion)

Figure 4.2 Interpretation test

Recall and Multiple Choice Tests

Lee (2002) conducted a study to assess learners' comprehension of what they read and their ability to process input for future-tense morphology. Two measures of comprehension were used in this study: free-written recall test and multiple-choice questions (see Figure 4.3).

1. Recall as much of what you just read as you can. Write in English. The emphasis is on how much you can remember.

2. Multiple-Choice Comprehension Questions
Please answer all of the following comprehension questions by selecting the answer that was given in the passage you read.

i. Sixty percent of developed countries ________ on telecommunications.
a. will depend b. already depend c. do not depend d. used to depend

ii. Telecommuting or teleworking ___________ frequently.
a. is not practised b. is already practised c. used to be practised d. will be practised

iii. A professional __________ work to any part of the world using telematics technologies.
a. already sends b. cannot yet send c. will send d. has been able to send

iv. Some sociologists claim that these technologies ________ social isolation.
a. generate b. cannot generate c. will generate d. have already generated

v. Some sociologists claim that these technologies ________ the human need for personal contact.
a. will influence b. already influence c. cannot yet influence d. have influenced

vi. Man, Homo sapiens, __________ Homo electronicus.
a. is already b. has become c. cannot become d. will become

Figure 4.3 Comprehension measure (from Lee, 2002)

Learners were asked to read a passage and immediately after to write everything they could remember from the passage in English. Correct recalls scored one point. One point was given to all target verbs correctly recalled with a future meaning. Following the recalls, the readers completed multiple-choice questions in English (see Figure 4.3). Each question had a blank (target verb) in it, and underneath the sentence learners had four choices. The choices rendered the verb in the past, present perfect, present or future, and learners were asked what the correct choice was.

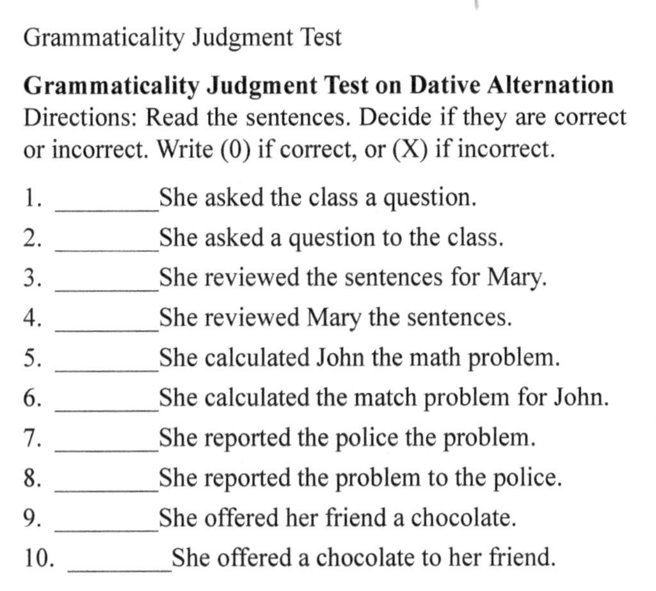

Grammaticality Judgment Test

Grammaticality Judgment Test on Dative Alternation
Directions: Read the sentences. Decide if they are correct or incorrect. Write (0) if correct, or (X) if incorrect.

1. ________She asked the class a question.
2. ________She asked a question to the class.
3. ________She reviewed the sentences for Mary.
4. ________She reviewed Mary the sentences.
5. ________She calculated John the math problem.
6. ________She calculated the match problem for John.
7. ________She reported the police the problem.
8. ________She reported the problem to the police.
9. ________She offered her friend a chocolate.
10. ________She offered a chocolate to her friend.

Figure 4.4 Grammaticality Judgment Test (from Fotos and Ellis 1991)

Fotos and Ellis (1991) conducted a study on the acquisition of a specific linguistic feature (dative alternation) using a Grammaticality Judgment task. Ten verbs were selected on the basis of observed errors in student usage, and a Grammaticality Judgment test of 20 sentences (20 points maximum score), 2 per verb, was designed (see Figure 4.4 below).

Tests judge actual experiences of persons doing tasks that they are likely to do in real life. All tests need to be thoroughly evaluated before they are used. The discussion of tasks and criteria for assessment is in fact a key contribution to achieving a valid and reliable testing procedure. Reliability can be defined as consistency of measurement and is a measure of the degree to which a test gives the same results when it is given on different occasions or when different people use it. When developing a test, the researcher would need to consider the following issues to ensure validity:

1. Take enough samples of behaviour.
2. Do not allow candidates too much freedom.
3. Write unambiguous items.
4. Ensure that tests are well laid out and perfectly legible.
5. Candidates should be familiar with format and testing techniques.

6. Provide uniform and non-distracting conditions of administration.
7. Develop detailed scoring procedure.

Online tests are also used in experimental research. In sentence matching tasks, for instance, two stimulus sentences are presented to the taker, one after another and for a very brief period of time, on a computer monitor. The first sentence appears on the left of the screen, and the second appears on the right of the screen. The first stimulus pair remains on screen for a short period of time and then a second member of a stimulus pair appears while a timer starts to measure time of responses. The participants' task is to determine whether the first and the second stimuli are identical or not. When they make a decision they press one of two buttons. At that point, the timer is stopped and the reaction time is registered. Psycholinguistic software is also available (see Chapter 7 in this book) to measure the speed of oral responses. Participants speak their responses to stimuli into a microphone which is connected to the computer's internal clock via a voice activator.

4.2.2 Data Analysis

In the experimental research framework, different designs imply different methods of statistical analysis. However, the main goal in experimental research is to demonstrate that two or more sets of pre-test scores show no difference between groups, and post-test scores show a statistical relevant difference.

Descriptive statistics are measurements of central tendency (mean and mode). The mean is the average value of our data. To calculate the mean, all the scores of each group are added up and the sum is divided by the total number of scores for a given set. An example: data were collected in the form of scores on a performance test (6 people (*N*) with the following scores: 4-8-3-6-5-4). In order to calculate the mean we add up all six individual scores and divide them by the number of participants (4+8+3+6+5+4 = 30/6 = mean = 5). The mode is the score that occurs with the highest frequency in the data set (in the case of the data set above, the mode = 4). Standard deviation (SD) indicates how much the data deviate from the mean. In order to calculate this variance the mean is first subtracted from every score in the data set:

$4–5 = −1$
$8–5 = 3$
$3–5 = −2$

6–5 = 1
5–5 = 0
4–5 = −1

Each difference is squared and then all the squares are added up:

1 + 9 + 4+ 1+ 0 + 1 = 16 (sum of squares)

The sum of squares is then divided by $N - 1$:

16/5 = 3.2 (variance)

The standard deviation (SD) is the square root of the variance: 1.79.

Parametric statistics is used to test hypotheses. The most common way of comparing the performance of two groups is through a statistical procedure called a *t*-test. The procedure (parametric statistics) is used to compare the means of two groups and helps to determine that the statistical difference between two groups is not due to chance. *T*-test procedures can be applied to the same sample (comparing means from the same data set/group from pre-test to post-test) or they can be used for independent samples (comparing the means of two different groups). The statistical analysis procedure provides the researcher with a *T-value* which is entered in a table which indicates whether the *T-value* of the two groups is statistically significant.

When the performance of more than two groups' means is compared and measured statistically, an ANOVA parametric procedure is adopted (*ANOVA)*. The two most common *ANOVA* procedures are: One-way *ANOVA* and Two-way *ANOVA*.

ANOVA analyzes a number of quantitative variables (dependent and independent variables, treatments and tests). In the case of One-way *ANOVA* a single factor is analyzed among three or more groups (e.g. type of treatment). Two-way *ANOVA* is used when more than one independent factor is considered (e.g. type of interaction and type of task).

The analysis results in an *F-value*, which is entered in a table to establish whether the *F-value* is significant. When the F-value is significant the researcher rejects the null hypothesis of no difference between treatments and therefore establishes the existence of some statistical relevant differences in the groups (i.e. at least one group is different).

In Table 4.1 the results of an *ANOVA* are graphically presented. The most important values is the *p*-value which if it is smaller than $p = 0.05$ (required significant level) would indicate that there is a statistical difference between the treatment groups.

Table 4.1 One-way *ANOVA*

ANOVA					
Source of variation	*SS*	*df*	*MS*	*F*	p-*value*
Between groups	80.22445	2	35.09998	1.240044	0.01
Within groups	1203.734	42	27.00092		
Total	1201.911	44			

TASK

Read Benati and Lee (2010) and answer these questions:

1. What was the purpose of the study (academic importance)?
2. What was the research framework used?
3. What were the main findings and their significance?
4. What are the main implications?
5. What are the limitations of the study?
6. What further research needs to be carried out?

Figure 4.5 Task

ANOVA indicates whether there are significant statistical differences between groups, but not what these differences are. To determine which instructional treatment is better than another, a different statistical analysis needs to be carried out. *Post-hoc* range tests (e.g. *Tukey Test*, *Scheffe Test*) can determine which means differ from each other. These statistical tests identify homogeneous sub-sets of means that are not different from each other and yield a matrix where asterisks indicate significantly different group means at an alpha level of 0.05 (the numerical measure of significance as in the case of the *ANOVA*).

Frequency is another measure in second language research which indicates how often a phenomena occurs (e.g. how often a particular group behaves). Frequency is used to count the number of occurrences (e.g. how often a learners make a particular error, how often a teacher provide feedback in the form of recast, etc.). Correlation is also used to determine possible relationships between and among variables but not necessarily the cause of that relationship. Most of the analysis techniques used in applied linguistics can be carried out with a computer and a number of statistical packages (SPSS) have been designed and are available (Larson-Hall 2010).

4.3 What Are the Key Advantages and Disadvantages?

According to Long (1984), the experimental research framework is the strongest research design available to evaluate a number of phenomena related to classroom language learning and language teaching. Experimental research is good at isolating and examining specific factors (Shadish, Cook and Campbell 2002: 2). There are different ways of carrying out an experiment; however, the design has to be constructed so that a number of variables can be controlled and manipulated and at the same time a methodologically rigorous procedure is developed.

The main purpose of research methodology is to make the research design as effective and valid as possible. The main goal is to make sure that the results of the study we have conducted are valid both internally and externally (Mackey and Gass 2005: 109). What does this mean? Internal invalidity of findings occurs when the findings might have been affected by other factors. External invalidity is when the results cannot be extended or applied to outside contexts. In order to make a valid comparison between groups, experimental designs require that other factors, called 'threats', do not interfere. Griffee (2004) defines a 'threat' as a condition which blinds or misleads research when they interpret their results. In order to make a study internally valid we need to be able to demonstrate that the relationship between the independent and dependent variables is unambiguous and not explained by other variables. Controlling factors such as individual differences might help the researcher to argue that those factors are not responsible for the effects of instruction on language learning, for instance.

The first internal factors that might invalidate research findings are the characteristics and size of participants in an experimental study. The characteristics of the subjects and the number of students involved are two important factors researchers need to take into consideration when they embark in a classroom study. Sometimes it is assumed that the population involved in a research project is representative of the general population to which the research applies. However, participants in a group are affected by many variables (e.g. attitude, motivation, gender, age, proficiency). The question that needs to be addressed before researchers start collecting data is: Are the groups representative samples of the same population? In order to equally distribute subject variables to groups, a random procedure might be used so that we can claim that the subject variables are divided by random chance. Alternatively, a matching procedure can be used to match subjects to groups in terms of the factors we believe might have an impact on the results of the study. The size of subject population could also be a factor influencing the validity and reliability of the results. Small populations magnify the effects of individual variability; the greater the size, the smaller the effect of individual variability. The characteristics of the population are also a matter of external validity as findings needs to be applied and generalized to situations outside those in which the research was conducted. The questions that needs to be addressed are: Can the findings obtained in a study be applied to a different population? Can the effects of an instructional treatment on school-age learners be generalized to adults? Conceptual replication studies are needed in order to generalize findings.

A second internal factor is history. History can be described as events other than the experimental treatment that can happen during the experiment and of which the researcher is not aware. These events can provide a different explanation of the effects obtained in a study. For instance, participants might have received additional instruction during the instructional period. This could cause a threat to a research hypothesis that states that innovation during investigation caused learners' improvement. This threat can be addressed by reducing the time needed to collect data and collect information about learners' habits and experience outside classroom time.

A third internal factor is the calculation of the time needed for data collection. How can I establish how much time is needed to show an effect for a treatment? There is no hard and fast rule for deciding when enough time has been given to collecting a valid sample of data. It is relative to factors such as context, amount of available time, sensitivity of the instruments used to elicit data, cognitive abilities of the groups, etc. The instruments used to collect data could also influence internal validity. Sometimes instruments (task sensitivity) are used as a tool to obtain information about the status of the subject (pre-test used before the experiment). However,

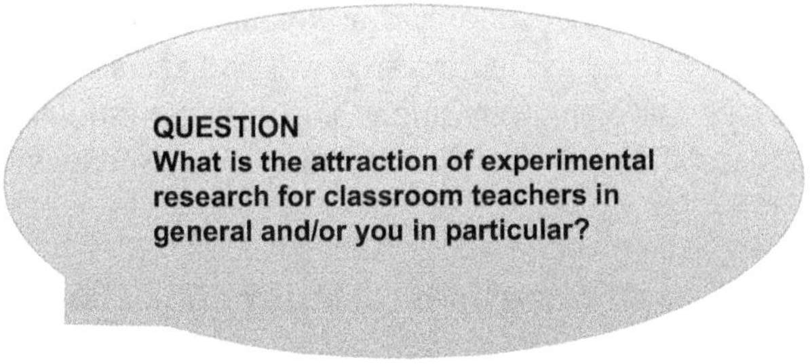

QUESTION
What is the attraction of experimental research for classroom teachers in general and/or you in particular?

Figure 4.6 Question

the pre-test could affect the internal validity of the experiment as learners can become test-wise and this practice might affect the participants' performance. To control for testing affect, two forms of the same test can be used (A and B). In the first instance, some participants take form A while others take form B. On a second instance, the participants who took form A now take form B, while the other participants take form A instead of form B. Using a control group which receives no treatment also addresses this issue, as any practice effect that exists should be reflected in pre-test/post-test differences of the control group.

Another possible threat for both internal and external validity is the so-called 'Hawthorne effect'. If participants are aware that they are in a special study, they may be affected by the attention they receive and this can cause for them to act differently than they normally would. One possible solution is to conduct the experiment in an unobtrusive way so that participants are not aware they are being studied.

The descriptive explicitness of the independent variable is also a very important factor to be controlled by the researcher. It is crucial to be able to describe the instructional treatment (independent variable) as explicitly as possible, providing details of how the way the treatment is implemented.

Teacher effect could also pose a threat, particularly if different teachers are used in an experimental study (one for the control group and a different one for the experimental group, for example). One teacher might be more proficient than the other. One possible solution is to use the same teacher for both groups and perhaps avoid the situation where the teacher is also the researcher.

The interaction of subject selection and research is an external factor which may influence the findings of an experimental study. Very often volunteers have to be used to collect data. The question which needs to be addressed is: To what degree do paid or volunteer subjects represent the general population to which the research will be generalized? It could be said for instance that volunteers might have a better attitude towards an experiment than existing subjects participating in an experiment.

4.4 What Does an Experimental Study Look Like?

In this section a typical experimental study is presented (Benati and Lee 2010). The intent is to show to readers how an experimental study is conducted in the language classroom and describe how the findings are presented. Experimental studies are reported in the literature as book chapters or journal articles. Normally they include the following main sections:

Purpose of the study
Research questions
Design and procedures

TASK

Read the two studies listed below and identify the following:

1. Research question/motivation of the study
2. Participants
3. Procedures
4. Materials
5. Assessment instruments and scoring procedure
6. Main findings

Benati, A. (2005). The effects of processing instruction, traditional instruction and meaning–output instruction on the acquisition of English simple past tense. *Language Teaching Research* 9(1), 67–113.

Toth, P. (2006). Processing instruction and a role for output in second language acquisition. *Language Learning* 56(2), 319–385.

Figure 4.7 Task

Results
Discussion and conclusion
References

The title of the study is: "Exploring the effects of processing instruction on discourse-level interpretation tasks with English past tense".

Purpose of the Study

This truly experimental study (Benati and Lee 2010) examined the acquisition of the English simple past tense. This linguistics feature is formed by adding the morpheme *-ed* to the end of verbs. The main purpose of this study was to determine if L2 learners receiving an approach to grammar instruction called 'processing instruction' may improve their ability to interpret the English past tense marker *-d* as measured by a discourse-level interpretation task. No previous research, within this framework, had measured the effects of processing instruction utilizing interpretation discourse-level tasks. To make this determination, the effects of processing instruction were compared to those of traditional grammar instruction.

Research Questions

The study was informed by two main questions:

Q1. Would learners receiving processing instruction and traditional instruction improve in their ability to interpret English past tense forms presented in sentences?

Q2. Would learners receiving processing instruction and traditional instruction improve in their ability to interpret English past tense forms embedded in discourse presented as a dialogue?

Design and Procedures

Participants

Three groups of participants, numbering 29 in the final data pool, participated in this study. They were all native speakers of Chinese who were learning English in a Chinese primary school. To select the population the following set of criteria were used in this study:

1. all participants had to be native speakers of Chinese;
2. they all had to be beginning-level learners of English; and,
3. they should not have been taught or should not have been previously exposed to the target linguistic feature (English simple past tense marker *–ed*) inside or outside the classroom.

The initial subject pool of 38 was further reduced to 29 subjects as only subjects who scored less than 50% of the maximum score on the pre-tests, both the sentence-level and discourse-level interpretation tasks, were included in the final data pool.

Procedures

A pre-test/post-test procedure was adopted. Pre-tests were administered a few weeks prior to the beginning of the treatment. Then subjects were randomly assigned to one of the following three groups: processing instruction (n = 10), traditional grammar instruction (n = 9) and a control group (n = 10). The same instructor delivered both instructional treatments and acted as facilitator during the treatment phases. Due to curriculum constraints, durative effects were not examined. Two tests were developed for this study: one interpretation sentence-level interpretation test and one discourse-level interpretation test. Pre-testing and post-testing combined lasted approximately 30 minutes. The instructional treatment lasted approximately six hours for the two groups. During the treatment period, feedback on performance was limited to telling participants whether an answer was right or wrong. No further explanation was offered and students seemed satisfied with the limited feedback. Limiting the feedback was consistent across the two groups. An immediate post-test was then carried out at the end of the second day of instruction. One-way ANOVAs were conducted on the raw scores for all pre-tests to assess whether there were any statistically significant differences among the three groups before the beginning of the experimental period. Repeated-measures ANOVAs were used on pre-test/post-test measures to assess whether there were any relevant effects for Treatment (instructional group) and Time (pre-test score vs post-test score).

Instructional Materials (Independent Variable)

The two sets of materials were balanced in terms of number of activities and vocabulary. The activities were constructed using highly frequent lexical items because of the age and beginning-level proficiency of the participants. The goal of processing instruction is to help learners alter their reliance on lexical items (Lexical Preference Principle) so that they process the target verb morpheme accurately and efficiently. The practical component of processing instruction consisted of structured input activities, both referential and affective activities. The practical component of traditional grammar instruction consisted of output-focused practices, mechanical and meaningful. The control group did not receive instruction on the target form during the treatment period but was exposed a comparable amount of exposure to the target language during their class time. The traditional grammar instruction group received explicit information on the past tense in English. This was a paradigmatic explanation of the target feature. The explicit information in the processing group focused on providing participants with information about the target feature and also about the specific processing problem addressed in this investigation.

Tests and Scoring Procedures (Dependent Variable)

In order to address the question raised in the present study, the tests consisted of two interpretation tests: sentence-level and discourse-level. Two versions of each test were created. The sentence-level interpretation test consisted of 20 items for which learners indicated temporal reference or were offered the option of not knowing (cannot tell). Ten of the items were distracters in that they used a present tense form for which the correct answer would be "right now". These items were not scored. The 10 target items on which learners were scored contained the targeted linguistic item, past tense *-d*. In the interpretation task learners were required to listen to sentences in which there were no temporal adverbs so that learners could not rely on them to assign tense. Instead the learners would have to rely on verbal morphology to indicate when the action took place (present or past temporal reference). To the extent possible, we designed the interpretation tasks to tap real-time comprehension. To that end, we allowed only a short gap of five seconds between questions for learners to mark their answers. For this interpretation measure raw scores were calculated so that a correct answer received one point and any incorrect answer would receive no points. The maximum score possible would, therefore, be 10 points for the sentence-level interpretation test (either pre-test or post-test).

The discourse-level interpretation test required learners to interpret past tense markers for verbs that were embedded in discourse. It consisted of a dialogue, which was spoken at a normal conversational speed by native speakers of English. The dialogue was recorded and played to the learners. No repetition was provided so the test would measure real-time comprehension. The dialogue contains many verbs but we selected 20 for the test. Ten of these were target forms in the past tense. The other 10 were in the present tense. Neither set of verbs co-occurred with a temporal adverb or any other reference to time. Learners were asked to decide whether the verb listed referred to present or past events. There were given one point for each correct assignment of the 10 target forms (past tense markers). The distracters (present markers) were not scored. As in the case of the interpretation sentence-level interpretation test, the pre-test and post-test were balanced in terms of difficulty and vocabulary. Learners ticked the answer sheet after listening to the whole dialogue.

Results

Sentence-level Interpretation Test

Pre-tests were administered to the students a few weeks before the beginning of the instructional treatment period. It is important to establish that there were no pre-existing differences between the processing instruction, the traditional instruction and the control groups so that we can attribute any post-treatment differences to the effects of instruction. The one-way ANOVA conducted on the interpretation pre-test for the simple past tense revealed no significant differences between the groups' mean scores before the treatment period, $F(2, 29) = .643, p = .534$. The means for the learners' scores on the interpretation sentence-level interpretation test for simple past tense, both pre- and post-tests, are presented in Table 4.2. The means indicate an improvement for the processing instruction group but not for either the traditional grammar instruction group or the control group.

These scores were submitted to a repeated-measures ANOVA for which Instruction (processing instruction, traditional grammar instruction and the control group) was the between-subjects factor and Time (pre-test vs post-test scores) was the within-subject factor (the repeated-measure). The statistical analysis yielded a significant main effect for Instruction, $F(2, 29) = 115.252, p = .000$, for Time, $F(2, 29) = 88.013, p = .000$, and a significant interaction between Instruction and Time, $F(1, 26) = 42.418, p = .000$. A post-hoc analysis showed that the processing instruction group performed significantly better on the post-test than the traditional grammar instruction group ($p = .000$) and the control group ($p = .000$). There was, however, no significant difference between the scores of the traditional grammar instruction group and the control group ($p = .625$)

Table 4.2 Descriptive statistics – sentence-level interpretation test

	Pre-test			*Immediate post-test*	
Variable	*N*	*Mean*	*SD*	*Mean*	*SD*
PI	10	1.00	1.054	5.30	0.823
TI	9	0.66	0.707	1.10	0.670
Control	10	0.60	0.699	0.60	0.699

Table 4.3 Descriptive statistics – discourse-level interpretation test

	Pre-test			*Immediate post-test*	
Variable	*N*	*Mean*	*SD*	*Mean*	*SD*
PI	10	2.80	0.918	8.10	1.197
TI	9	2.10	0.781	2.30	0.866
Control	10	1.80	1.032	1.80	0.198

Discourse-level Interpretation Test

The means and standard deviations for the interpretation discourse-level interpretation test are presented in Table 4.3. A one-way ANOVA on the pre-test scores of the three groups to insure that there were no pre-existing differences between the groups was adopted. The results showed no significant differences between the three groups' mean scores before instruction ($F(2,29) = 3.073$, $p = .063$). The groups possessed equivalent knowledge of the English marker *-d* before receiving instruction on the English past tense marker. Any differences we find among post-test scores will be attributed to the effects of instruction. A repeated-measures ANOVA to compare the effects of Instruction and Time and the interaction between Instruction and Time was used. As in the case of the sentence-level interpretation test, the statistical analysis revealed a significant main effect for Instruction ($F(2,29) = 107.734$, $p = .000$), a significant main effect for Time $F(2,29) = 97.290$, $p= .000$), and a significant interaction between Time and Instruction $F(2,29) = 55.751$, $p = .000$) . The post-hoc test carried out on the post-test scores of the three groups revealed that the processing instruction group's performance was statistically higher than that of the traditional grammar instruction group (p = .001) and the control group (p = .001). No significant difference was found between the scores of the traditional and the control groups ($p = .063$)

Discussion and Conclusion

The results provide positive answers to the two questions formulated at the beginning of this study and support the two hypotheses.

The first two questions of this study were formulated to investigate the effects of processing instruction and traditional grammar instruction on the interpretation of sentences containing the target feature (past tense markers *-d*). The results of the statistical analysis clearly indicate that the processing instruction group improved from pre-test to post-test on the

TASK
Find a published research article that you believe used a truly experimental or quasi-experimental method. Download, copy or print the article, and answer the following questions:

1. What do you find in the article that tells you the design was truly experimental or quasi-experimental?
2. Where did the research take place, and who were the students?
3. Can you identify the dependent and independent variables?
4. What are the main findings? Has this study provided an answer to the questions raised?
5. Can we consider this study valid and reliable? If yes, why?
6. What is the next step? Can you indicate other possible avenues for further research?

Figure 4.8 Task

interpretation sentence-level interpretation test. The performance of the processing instruction group was statistically significant and superior to the performance of the traditional and control groups.

The second research question was formulated to investigate the effects of processing instruction on a discourse-level interpretation task. The results of the statistical analyses presented in the previous section have clearly shown that the processing instruction treatment made significant improvement from pre-test to post-test as measured by the discourse-level interpretation task. The performance of the processing instruction group was statistically significantly different to the performance of the traditional and the control groups.

The results in this experimental research have confirmed the overall findings obtained by all studies investigating the effects of processing instruction at the sentence level. These studies have unanimously indicated that processing instruction is a very effective instructional treatment. In addition to that, this study provides additional support for the view that processing instruction is an effective instructional treatment in enhancing learners' ability to interpret a target form when it is embedded in discourse. One of the limitations of the present study is the small number of participants in each group. Future research should address this limitation. Another area for future research is to examine discourse-level effects over a longer period of time.

4.5 What Are the Key Terms?

Analysis of Variance (ANOVA) is a statistical procedure used to measure the statistical differences between two or more groups.

Assessment (tests) is the dependent variable used to measure the effects of the independent variable (instructional treatment(s)).

Control group is a group of participants used for comparison purposes. Unlike in the case of the experimental group, no treatment is administered to the control group.

Descriptive statistics are measurements of frequency, central tendency, standard deviation and standard error.

Dependent variable is a factor which might be affected by other variables (independent) manipulated by the researcher.

Experimental group is the treatment group (independent variable), the group of participants with whom the innovative treatment is applied.

Independent variable is a variable introduced by the researcher to measure its effects on the dependent variable.

Mean refers to the average of a set of scores.

One-shot design is a very basic design and involves the use of a single treatment, a single group and a single post-test.

Parametric statistics is a family of statistical procedures that requires normal distribution and a continuous scale (*t*-test, *ANOVA*).

Pre-test is a test that is administered before the beginning of the experimental period.

Post-test is a test that is the same or very similar to the pre-test, and is administered immediately at the end of the experimental period or after to measure delayed effects.

***p*-value** is the statistical value that stands for probability. It provides statistical information of whether there is a difference between the score of two of more groups. If the p-value is small (the coefficient is .05 or smaller) then we can make the claim that there is statistical difference between groups. If the coefficient is higher than .05, the groups are statistically similar and therefore we can't claim that a statistical difference exists.

Quasi-experimental design is a very economical design as it allows the use existing groups rather than assigning participants to groups through a randomization or matching procedure.

Random assignment is a type of placement that refers to the process by which any participant has an equal chance to be assigned to any group. One method of random assignment is to write names on pieces of paper, put them into a container, and have somebody draw them out one by one without seeing the names. Another way is to use a computer program that can randomize a list of names or numbers.

Standard deviation indicates how much the data deviates from the mean.

Truly experimental design involves the use of two or more groups which have been formed through a process of randomization.

4.6 What Are the Key Readings?

Benati, A. (2005). The effects of processing instruction, traditional instruction and meaning–output instruction on the acquisition of English simple past tense. *Language Teaching Research*, *9*(1), 67–93. http://dx.doi.org/10.1191/1362168805lr154oa

Benati, A. & Lee, J. (2008). *Grammar Acquisition and Processing Instruction: Secondary And Cumulative Effects*. Clevedon: Multilingual Matters.

Benati, A., & Lee, J. (2010). Exploring the effects of processing instruction on discourse-level interpretation tasks with English past tense. In A. Benati & J. Lee. *Processing Instruction and Discourse*, (pp. 178–197). London: Continuum.

Cook, T.D., & Campbell, D.T. (1979). *Quasi Experimentation: Design and Analytical Issues for Field Settings*. Chicago, IL: Rand McNally.

Griffee, D. (2004). Research tips: Validity and history. *Journal of Developmental Education*, *28*(1), 1–38.

Larson-Hall, J. (2010). *A Guide to Doing Statistics in Second Language Research Using SPSS*. London: Routledge.

Lee, J. (2002). The incidental acquisition of Spanish future tense morphology through reading in a second language. *Studies in Second Language Acquisition*, *24*(1), 55–80. http://dx.doi.org/10.1017/S0272263102001031

Long, M. (1984). Process and product in ESL program evaluation. *TESOL Quarterly, 18*(3), 409–425. http://dx.doi.org/10.2307/3586712

Mackey, A., & Gass, S. (2005). *Second Language Research: Methodology and Design*. Mahwah, NJ: Erlbaum.

Rasinger, S. (2013). *Quantitative Research in Linguistics*. London: Bloomsbury.

Seliger, H., & Shohamy, E. (1989). *Second Language Research Methods*. Oxford: Oxford University Press.

Shadish, W., & Luellen, J. (2006). Quasi-experimental design. In J.L. Green, G. Camilli, & P.B. Elmore (Eds.), *Handbook of Complementary Methods in Education Research*, (pp. 539–550). Mahwah, NJ: Erlbaum.

Shadish, W., Cook, T., & Campbell, D. (2002). *Experimental and Quasi-Experimental Designs for Generalized Causal Inference*. Boston, MA: Houghton Mifflin.

Toth, P. (2006). Processing instruction and a role for output in second language acquisition. *Language Learning, 56*(2), 319–385. http://dx.doi.org/10.1111/j.0023-8333.2006.00349.x

Wei, L., & Moyer, M. (Eds.). (2008). *The Blackwell Guide to Research Methods in Bilingualism and Multilingualism*. Oxford: Blackwell.

5 Classroom Observation Research Framework

Chapter Preview

In this chapter the basic concept and components of the classroom observation research framework will be presented. What is classroom observation? Why do we carry out classroom observation? How can we carry out classroom observation? These are some of the key questions addressed in this chapter. Key procedures to collect and analyze data within an observation research framework will be discussed. The advantages and disadvantages of using this framework will be explored. An exemplary observation classroom-based study will be presented to show readers how such as study is conducted and how findings are presented. Key terms associated with observation research and sources for further reading will be provided at the end of the chapter.

5.1 What Are the Key Concepts and Components?

Despite the fact that observation is a natural source of human knowledge, it is not always a reliable tool, as people often tend to see what they expect to see in an observable phenomena. When things are observed we might or might not always capture everything that is in front of our eyes. However, over the years, teachers and researchers have very often been inspired to develop their research projects by what they have observed in the language classroom. Observation has been one of the key vehicles for very insightful research, and observing classroom behaviour (through watching, listening and recording) has provided important answers and insights into key questions/issues in second language acquisition. In second language research, observation is frequently used as an alternative to a formal experiment. An observation documents life inside the classroom. However, an observation study is different from an experimental study on three counts: assumptions, methods/procedures and attitudes to evidence. In an experimental study the researcher investigates the possible relationship between an independent and a dependent variable. Experiments are analytical and hypothesis-driven. They tend to investigate individual pieces of the language learning puzzle and are informed by specific questions and hypotheses formulated on the basis of previous empirical research findings and the review of theoretical accounts.

Observations are synthetic and data-driven approaches to second language research. In an observation study, a researcher will investigate a phenomenon in its entirety, the whole of the language learning puzzle. In other words, this research framework is data-driven as the observer needs to collect enough data to be able to formulate a hypothesis or a question as a result of the analysis of the data collected.

Classroom observation belongs to the naturalistic tradition in its attempt to investigate language behaviour in the natural context in which it occurs. It involves the study of the characteristics of a group in the real world and the researcher makes no attempt to isolate or manipulate a phenomena under investigation. Insights and generalizations emerge from close contact with the data rather than from a theory of language learning and use. In an observation the observer must consider three issues:

1. How the observation takes place (role of the observer and/or teacher). The main question is: Is the researcher planning to observe another teacher's class or observing his/her own class?
2. What observation items the research adopts (open or closed items). Using open items means that the observer has not determined exactly what he/she is looking for. With the use of closed items, the observer has decided what he/she is looking for. The main questions are: Does the observer know what he/she would like to observe (in which case the observer should develop and make use of closed items)? Or is the observer starting with no predetermined categories (in which case the observer can develop and make use of open items)?
3. How the data is collected and analyzed. The data gathered may be quantitative (for example, frequency counts) or qualitative, for example, verbal descriptions. The main question is: Is the observer planning to collect data in numbers or words?

TASK
Describe a time when you observed something about your teaching or something that happened in your class that you thought was interesting.

Figure 5.1 Task

To summarize, the main principles of the observation research framework are:

- Observation studies are normally conducted in the context in which the participants study and/or work.
- Observation studies allow the observer to study a behaviour in its natural context.
- The observer tends to avoid any manipulations of the phenomena under investigation.
- Generalizations and hypotheses usually emerge during the course of data collection and interpretation (data-driven approach).
- It is a qualitative and process-oriented research framework, but a more quantitative element (product component) can be incorporated.

Classroom observation is an ideal methodological framework to systematically investigate teaching and learning issues and processes in a second language classroom context. Classroom observation is used in second language research for different goals: to compare language teaching methods; to explore effective classroom pedagogical approaches; to evaluate teachers and materials, etc. All these issues are fundamental components of classroom research to investigate what actually happens inside the classroom.

5.2 What Are the Key Data Collection and Analysis Procedures?

How can we carry out classroom observation? Successful observation requires something more than just sitting and watching in a language classroom. Observation is the act of watching something and recording the results in a way that produces data that can subsequently be analyzed and interpreted. The observation items which the observer decides to observe might be *open* or *closed* in nature.

Open means that the observer does not specify in advance what exactly the items under observation are. In this case, the observer is interested in observing what is happening, but he/she has not determined exactly what are the key factors under observation. He/she might notice new things which were not considered at the beginning of the research.

Closed means that the items under observation are specified in advance by the researcher. *Closed* means the observer has decided what he/she is looking for. More structured observation procedures are adopted.

The data gathered may be quantitative, for example frequency counts, or qualitative, for example verbal descriptions. There are a number of observational techniques utilized within this research framework. In this section a variety of data collection observation procedures will be described.

5.2.1 Basic Observation Record Sheet(s)

The basic observation record sheet is a tool which can be used to keep a record about the context and the details of a classroom observation session. In each sheet (see example in Figure 5.2), the observer is able to record two

Context Date: Place: Teacher: Class/level: Number of students: Course goals and objectives:
Observation General account of what happened, with times: **Evaluation**

Figure 5.2 Basic Observation Record Sheet

Instances	1	2	3	4	5	6	7	8	9	10
Type of feedback										
Recast										
Explicit error correction										
Metalinguistic clues										
Clarification requests										
Self-correction										

Figure 5.3 Checklist

types of data. The first type of data is contextual, as it includes information such as date, place, teacher's name, and other useful background information (first row of the record sheet). The second type of data consists of the actual record of the class and the evaluation (interpretation, comments and impressions) of the observer (second row of the record sheet).

The positive aspect to using this instrument is that the observer can observe specific materials, procedures and activities, and can evaluate them. However, two main disadvantages of using this procedure are the fact that it is laborious and that not everything in the classroom can be recorded in a clear way. Audio recording could represent a possible solution to these shortcomings as recording picks up the details that might otherwise be missed and/or go unnoticed. In the example in Figure 5.3 (Masson 2011), instances of feedback were recorded chronologically. High-inference categories (motivation, student learning styles, etc.) have to be carefully defined for the observer to be in the right position to collect the data. One of the challenges in observation studies is the length of time required to analyze data and the lack of tools available for conducting the analysis. One possible response to these challenges is for the observer to use categories he/she has decided in advance and prior to the observation of the data. The data can be analyzed using a category system.

5.2.2 Checklists

A checklist is an observation instrument with specific listed categories (closed items) that the observer intends to measure. The data collected is frequency data and captures details of the lesson observed. Checklists are used in combination with other data collection methods. A checklist is very effective with low-inference categories (How many error corrections from the teacher were there?) but not as useful with high inference categories which require more interpretation (Is the teacher using a communicative approach to grammar teaching?). In the example below, instances of feedback, clearly defined, were recorded numerically. The checklist (see Figure 5.3) had the number of possible instances on the right and the list of feedback on the left so that the observer could check how many times a particular kind of feedback was used.

Students or teachers' behaviour are documented, but this observation system does not indicate sequences or length of interaction.

5.2.3 Videotaped Lessons and Transcripts

Video recording of a lesson (partial or complete) is another technique used to collect data within the classroom observation framework. Video recording provides clear insights and detailed information about what is going on in the classroom. Video recording a lesson followed by the transcription of the lesson can reveal things that otherwise might not have been noticed by the observer. The recording procedures include a description of the recording schedule, equipment and information on data collection. Transcriptions provide very detailed evidence on particular aspects of classroom interaction and can be analyzed through coding and categorizing the key elements. Key elements are identified through the analysis of the transcripts where communalities, differences and specific patterns are identified.

5.2.4 Structured Observation

Structured observation is classroom observation that makes use of previously defined categories. There are many structured observation instruments available in second language research. Flanders (1970) developed a list of categories of teacher and learner behaviour associated with successful teaching. His interaction analysis system is called FIAC (Flanders' Interaction Analysis Categories) and contained the groups of categories shown in Figure 5.4.

Flanders used a tally sheet to mark every time the different categories were noted during observation. The tallies are recorded in a matrix which might or might not reveal some teaching patterns. A more sophisticated model is FLINT (Foreign Language Interaction), which includes a higher number of categories (see Figure 5.5 below).

TEACHER TALK

Indirect influence
- Accepts feeling
- Praises or encourages
- Accepts or uses ideas of student
- Asks questions

Direct influence
- Lecturing
- Giving directions
- Criticizing or justifying authority

STUDENT TALK
- Student-talk response
- Student talk-initiation
- Silence or confusion

Figure 5.4 FIAC categories

TEACHER TALK

Indirect influence
- Deals with feelings
- Praises or encourages
- Jokes
- Uses ideas of students
- Repeats student response verbatim
- Asks questions

Direct influence
- Gives information
- Corrects without rejection
- Gives directions
- Directs pattern drills
- Criticizes student's behaviour
- Criticizes student's response

STUDENT TALK
- Student response, specific
- Student response, choral
- Student response, open-ended or student-initiated
- Silence
- Confusion
- Laughter

Figure 5.5 FLINT categories

Fanselow (1987) developed another observation scheme for classroom research called FOCUS (Foci for Observing Communication Used in Settings). The scheme does not have separate categories for teachers and learners, but it proposes five characteristics of communication in settings:

- Who communicates?
- What is the pedagogical purpose of the communication?
- What mediums are used to communicate?
- How are the mediums used to communicate areas of content?
- What areas of content are communicated?

FOCUS is primarily based on the communicative competence model, defined by Canale (1983) as the integration of five basic competences:

- grammatical (grammar, lexicon and phonetics);
- sociolinguistic (communicative functions, appropriateness of grammatical forms);
- sociocultural (cultural concepts, attitudes, values);
- discourse (structure, coherence, cohesiveness); and
- strategic (language skills, mental operations, processes and strategies).

COLT (Communicative Orientation of Language Teaching), proposed by Fröhlich, Spada and Allen (1985), is also a classroom research system based on the analysis of classroom discourse. COLT was principally developed to measure the extent to which an instructional treatment was communicatively oriented and included the categories shown in Figure 5.6.

COLT was an observation system influenced by communicative approaches to language learning and teaching. It was designed for three reasons: to capture psycholinguistically valid categories for classroom observation; to investigate the communicative orientation of language practices; and to meet the needs for research on the relationship between learning and teaching. It comprises two parts: classroom activities and classroom language. Analysis of this system includes establishing a percentage of time spent on the individual categories in an attempt to demonstrate that communicative teaching facilitates effective learning.

Structured observation instruments are popular ways of collecting data in second language acquisition research, particularly when using low-inference categories which can offer reliable data. Structured observations are used to observe and systematically analyze what is going on in the language classroom in order to capture key elements, factors and problems in language teaching and learning processes. In most observation schemes, the observer marks the sequence of an event (see Figure 5.7 adapted from Nunan 1989). Observation schemes have also high inference categories which require judgment (see Figure 5.8).

Part A: Classroom events

I. Activity/Episodes
II. Participant organization
III. Content
IV. Student modality
V. Materials

Part B: Communicative features

I. Use of target language
II. Information gap
III. Sustained speech
IV. Reaction to code or message
V. Incorporation of preceding utterances
VI. Discourse initiation
VII. Relative restriction of linguistic form

Figure 5.6 COLT categories

	Tallies	Total
1. Teacher asks a display question		
2. Teacher asks a referential question		
3. Teacher explains a grammatical point		
4. Teacher explains a meaningful vocabulary item		
5. Teacher gives an instruction		
6. Learner asks a question		
7. Learner answers a question		
8. Learner works in pair		

Figure 5.7 Tally sheet

	X low	low	fair	High	X high
Clarity (teacher)					
Comprehension (student)					
Depth (programme)					
Language skills					

Figure 5.8 TALOS: high inference

There are a number of advantages of using an observation scheme:

- comparability with other studies (large database);
- simplified analysis of data;
- measuring change over different time periods.

The two examples in Figures 5.7 and 5.8 are from observations schemes which adopt predetermined categories to observe and collect specific data (TALOS is a Target Language Observation Scheme, see Ullmann and Geva 1982). Students' and teachers' behaviour is documented and the frequency of types of behaviour is documented in real time (or with audio-videotape recordings), although the tally sheet does not indicate sequences or length of interaction.

MOLT (Motivational Orientation of Language Teaching) has been devised (Guilloteaux and Dörnyei 2008) to capture what instructors do to promote motivation among L2 learners. This observation scheme is based on the COLT scheme but uses categories (see Figure 5.9) of observable teachers' behaviour derived from Dörnyei's strategies framework for language classroom.

Teacher's motivational teaching practice

Teacher discourse
Participation structure
Encouraging, positive, respective self-evaluation
Activity design

Learners' motivated behaviour:

Attention students pay in class
Extent of their participation
Volunteering in tasks

Figure 5.9 Categories used for MOLT

TASK
Read three studies using different structured observation schemes and describe the following:

1. Observation procedures
2. Analysis
3. Findings

Figure 5.10 Task

Observation schemes are designed to meet the needs of research on relationships between learning and teaching.

5.2.5 Unstructured Observation

An alternative to a basic observation record sheet is in-class observation notes written after an event/classroom observation is over. A diary is a log or journal written mainly by the observer reflecting on the observations made. A diary has he following characteristics:

- It serves as a chronological account of the events observed.
- It serves as a source for descriptive data.
- It helps the observer to reflect on what happened.
- It provides recalled data to be analyzed.

Diaries are used in second language research for two main purposes:

1. to assist researchers in assessing their own learning processes (Schmidt and Frota 1986); in this case the same person collects and analyzes his/her data; and
2. to collect data to enable researchers to investigate and observe learning and teaching processes.

Diaries take the form of a standard notebook or single sheets of paper kept in a folder. Researchers decide to keep a diary and use it as a form of

TASK
Read Spada (1986) and answer these questions:

1. What was the purpose of the study (academic importance)?
2. What was the research framework used?
3. What were the main findings and their significance?
4. What are the main implications?
5. What are the limitations of the study?
6. What further research needs to be carried out?

Figure 5.11 Task

observation tool to assess the effectiveness of curriculum and pedagogy in language learning and teaching. An example might be a new course that is taught, where the researcher is interested in the evaluation and revision of that course.

A diary in this case is used to record teacher's and student's thoughts and feelings about the teaching and learning experience in order to identify a specific issue/topic/problem which needs to be examined. Again, the use of a diary is effective in collecting opinions, reflections, views and reactions from the participants and the teacher.

One of the advantages of using diaries is that the observer (diarist) and the participant can be the same person. This is often the case for research conducted in the classroom, where the teacher is the observer and one of the participants at the same time. The teacher-observer is using a diary to examine, observe and reflect on his/her research and practices in order to become aware of certain issues and then try to resolve them.

5.2.6 Ethnographic Analysis

Ethnographic analysis is an observational technique (Hammersley 1998) using material drawn from the first-hand experience of a fieldworker based in a natural setting, as opposed to artificial or experimental conditions. The ethnographic technique seeks to understand work environments and activities in a real-world context in a longitudinal approach (lengthy periods of time on site). Ethnographic studies observe and analyze participants' day-to-day social activities and social actions in their natural environment (e.g. home, workplace, public space, etc.). In doing so this technique does not make use of predetermined categories as this tends to focus the observer's attention in a particular direction, which might cause the researcher to miss something important which has not been categorized.

5.3 What Are the Key Advantages and Disadvantages?

Using observation procedures to collect data in the classroom is particularly useful for the researcher in terms of observing and directly evaluating teaching and learning issues in a specific language course, issues related to materials, and particular language tasks or practices. Observation of particular practices (e.g. use of language tasks and communicative grammar activities, use of target language, different feedback techniques) can lead the observer to formulate specific questions or hypotheses about possible relationships between learning and teaching, for example. Observation is also an effective methodological framework when the researcher is investigating specific features and more structured observation schemes are used (e.g. COLT, TALOS, etc.). Theses schemes can collect data observing specific predetermined categories, and produce numerical results which can be analyzed statistically. The teacher can be the observer of his/her own class, and this can be positive in terms of not having an external presence which might disrupt the behaviour of students and the language classroom dynamics.

There are a number of disadvantages of using observation which needs some reflection. First of all, not everything can be observed and recorded in the language classroom. Very often, depending on the observation procedures utilized, things might go unnoticed and not recorded. Second, the importance of the role of the observer must be considered. There are bias factors which need to be considered. An observer can interpret events/episodes through the lens of his/her own experience, assumptions and interests.

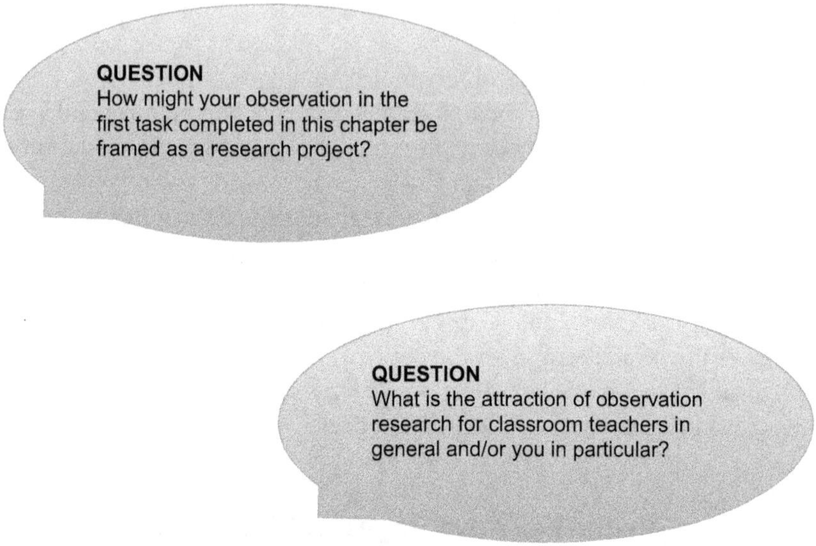

QUESTION
How might your observation in the first task completed in this chapter be framed as a research project?

QUESTION
What is the attraction of observation research for classroom teachers in general and/or you in particular?

Figure 5.12 Question

If the observer is also the classroom teacher, it is difficult to maintain his/her openness, as teachers would be familiar with teaching and specific characteristics of the class under observation. If the observer is not the usual classroom teacher, there is another threat: the observer can have an effect on the behaviour of the classroom or some of the participants.

5.4 What Does an Observation Study Look Like?

In this section an exemplary observation classroom-based study is presented (Gurzynski-Weiss and Révész 2012). The intent is to show readers how observation research is carried in the language classroom and describe the different components of this research methodological framework. The title of the study is "Tasks, teacher feedback, and learner modified output in naturally occurring classroom interaction" (Gurzynski-Weiss and Révész 2012).

Purpose of the Study

Despite the existing large research database on the role of tasks and interactional feedback, there is little research measuring the role of feedback and task factors during natural teacher-student classroom interaction. More specifically, this observation study investigates the amount, type and immediate use of teacher feedback in a language classroom context. In relation to the three factors the study explores the following: "whether feedback is provided during task versus nontask work; whether feedback occurs while students are engaged in focused versus unfocused tasks; and whether feedback is supplied in the pre-, during-, or possibly post-task phase" (Gurzynski-Weiss and Révész 2012: 853). The authors of the paper adopt the Ellis (2003: 10) definition of task, according to which tasks have six main properties: "A task (1) is a workplan, in other words, a planned activity; (2) involves primary attention to meaning; (3) entails real-world processes of language use, that is, leads to discourse similar to that encountered in real life; (4) requires the use of any of the four skills; (5) engages cognitive processes such as 'selecting, classifying, ordering, reasoning, and evaluating information'; and (6) has a nonlinguistic outcome, which provides the criteria in terms of which task completion may be assessed."

Design and Procedures

In order to measure whether feedback is provided during task or non-task work, whether feedback occurs while students perform focused versus unfocused tasks and whether feedback is supplied in the pre-, during- or post-task phase, data were collected from nine intermediate Spanish classes in the United States. The philosophy of the approach and programme used in these Spanish foreign language courses was highly communicative. Teachers in these classes had been required to enrol in a teaching methodology course which prepares the teachers in developing communicative tasks and discusses way to provide feedback to students in a meaning-based classroom.

Participants

Participants were all university students who were studying Spanish as part of the university programme, which required them to study a foreign language for four semesters. They were all intermediate students of Spanish between the ages of 18 and 22 and the nine classes comprised an average of 16 students each. Of the nine teachers observed, five were native speakers of Spanish and four were non-native.

Procedures for Data Collection

The authors videotaped the nine classes 23 times over a period of four days. The 23 50-minute classroom recordings were transcribed and coded by both researchers to ensure transcriptions and coding reliability.

The following procedures were used to code the recordings for task-related variables, feedback and modified output. For the task-related variables three mains steps were taken. First of all teaching activities identified in the transcripts were coded as tasks or non-tasks using the six criteria properties from Ellis (2003). The activities coded as non-tasks lacked a main focus on communication, did not have a communicative outcome and did not engage learners in the use of language communicative and real purposes. Second, the tasks were categorized in terms of focused (using specific features) or unfocused (prompting the use of specific constructions) type. Third, tasks observed were divided into pre-task, during-task and post-task phases.

In the case of coding the transcripts to capture feedback and modified output during teacher-student interaction, the researchers took the following steps. First of all, all the non-target-like utterances from the students were identified. Then all responses from the teachers were classified in terms of the following categories: recast, confirmation checks, clarification requests, repetitions, negotiation, elaborations, elicitations, metalinguistic feedback and overt corrections. These categories were subsequently classified as implicit or explicit responses. All but metalinguistic feedback and overt corrections were considered implicit feedback. Finally, the two researchers coded the transcripts considering feedback episodes as an opportunity for modified output: whether teachers provided learners with opportunities for modified output and whether learners modified their production immediately after teachers' feedback or not.

Based on four dependent variables (type and amount of feedback, opportunities and incidence of modified output) frequencies and percentages were calculated in relation to three main predictors (task, task focus, task phase). Statistical analysis (chi-square tests, logistic regression) were used to establish possible associations and to measure the relationships between the dependent and independent factors. Chi-square is a statistical test used in second language research to test the frequency of a dependent variable across categories of one or more independent variables. Logistic regression is a statistical method to test the possible influence of a number of independent variables on a dependent variable.

Results and Interpretation

Feedback and Modified Output During Task Versus Non-task Work

In the 23 lessons observed the two researchers identified 51 tasks (27 tasks and 24 non-tasks). In teacher-student interaction 384 errors were addressed with feedback. Recast and implicit feedback was more used and was more frequent (67%) than explicit feedback (33%). Students were given more opportunities for modified output in non-tasks than in tasks.

Feedback and Modified Output During Focused Versus Unfocused Tasks

Among the 27 tasks identified, 13 were focused and 14 were unfocused. A close qualitative analysis of the 13 tasks revealed the following task characteristics: 10 were structured-based production tasks, two were consciousness-raising tasks and one was a comprehension task. In addition to this data, the analysis showed the following: learners made more errors in unfocused tasks than in focus tasks; teachers provided more feedback during unfocused than in focused tasks; teachers made use of implicit feedback techniques (73%) more than explicit ones (27%) during focused tasks; and teachers gave learners more opportunity for output modification in focused tasks compared to unfocused tasks. There was no statistical association between occurrence of modified output and the type of task (focused or unfocused).

Feedback and Modified Output Across Task Phases

All the tasks identified in the transcripts (27) were divided into pre-task, during-task and post-task phases. Most of the errors were made by students in the post-task phase (221) and only one quarter were in the during-task phase (70). Learners received more feedback during the post-task phase. This feedback was more of the implicit type (80%) than the explicit type (20%), with recast being the most common type.

More opportunities to modify output were given in the during-task phase rather than in the post-task phase, but no statistical difference was found. No or very few errors, feedback and modified output opportunities were observed in the pre-task phase.

Conclusion

In Table 5.1 the main findings for the study are displayed. The key findings indicated the following patterns:

- During non-tasks teacher feedback was twice as likely to be provided.
- During non-tasks learners had more opportunity for output modifications.
- In unfocused tasks teachers were 60% more likely to provide feedback.
- Teachers' corrections entailed an opportunity for learners to modify their production in focused tasks more than in unfocused tasks.

Table 5.1 Summary of results (adopted from Gurzynski-Weiss and Révész 2012: 869)

Dependent variables	*Task vs non-task*	*Focused vs unfocused tasks*	*During-task vs post-task*
Amount of TF	more in non-tasks	more in unfocused	more in post-task
Type of TF	no difference	no difference	more implicit in post-task
Opportunity for MO	more in non-tasks	more in focused	no difference
Production of MO	more in non-tasks	no difference	no difference

Note: TF = teacher feedback; MO = modified output; "more" and "no difference" are based on the outcomes of Pearson's chi-square tests of independence followed up, where appropriate, by binary logistic regression analyses, given $p < .05$ and CI.95.

Teachers preferred to provide feedback in the post-task phase and use implicit techniques such as recast and overt corrections as opposed to explicit ones.The present study investigated teacher-student feedback patterns in relation to three task-related factors: task as compared to non-tasks; focused and unfocused tasks; and task phases. The results clearly indicated that non-tasks generated more feedback from the teachers and opportunities for learner output modifications. A possible explanation of these findings can be found in the differential communicative orientation of tasks and non-tasks. It was found that teachers were more likely to address errors with feedback during unfocused tasks, and students were given significantly more opportunities to produce modified output during focused tasks. It is suggested that teachers' "feedback behavior was in fact affected by the preplanned linguistic features embedded in focused tasks, in that teachers were likely to correct more frequently when learners committed errors in the linguistic feature the task was designed to elicit and provide practice on" (Gurzynski-Weiss and Révész 2012: 871).

Language teachers tend to use the post-task phase as a forum for focus on form to a greater extent than the during-task stage. Task factors may be significant moderator variables of the incidence and use of interactional feedback.

TASK
Read Lyster, R., & Ranta, L. (1997). Corrective feedback and learner uptake: Negotiation of form in communicative classrooms. *Studies in Second Language Acquisition*, 20. 51–81.
Answer the following questions:

1. What was the main purpose of the study?
2. What do you find in the article that tells you the design was observational in terms of the research framework?
3. What instruments were used?
4. What are the main findings? Has this study provided an answer to the questions raised?
5. Can we consider this study valid and reliable? If yes, why?
6. What is the next step? Can you indicate other possible avenues for further research?

Figure 5.13 Task

5.5 What Are the Key Terms?

Basic Observation Record Sheet refers to any type of written data collection made by an observer during a language class.

Checklist is a list of things that an observer is going to look at when observing a class. This list may have been prepared by the observer or the teacher or both. Observation checklists not only give an observer a structure and framework for an observation but also serve as a contract of understanding with the teacher, who may as a result be more comfortable, and will get specific feedback on aspects of the class.

Structured observations are systematic investigations that generate numerical data, for example, frequency of an event or behaviour, which are entered into an observation schedule.

Recording lessons and transcripts (audio recording or video recording) are procedures used to collect data in the classroom and capture planned and unplanned student-teacher interactions and tasks.

5.6 What Are the Key Readings?

Allen, P., Fröhlich, M., & Spada, N. (1984). The communicative orientation of language teaching: An observation scheme. In J. Handscombe, R. Orem, & B Taylor, (Eds.), *On TESOL '83: The Question of Control* (pp. 231–252). Washington, DC: TESOL.

Allwright, D. (1988). *Observation in the Language Classroom*. London: Longman.

Flanders, N. (1970). *Analyzing Teaching Behavior*. Reading, MA: Addison-Wesley Publications.

Fröhlich, M., Spada, N., & Allen, P. (1985). Differences in the communicative orientation of L2 classrooms. *TESOL Quarterly*, *19*, 27–57.

Guilloteaux, M., & Dörnyei, Z. (2008). Motivating language learners: A classroom-oriented investigation of the effects of motivational strategies on student motivation. *TESOL Quarterly*, *42*, 55–77.

Gurzynski-Weiss, L., & Révész, A. (2012). Tasks, teacher feedback, and learner modified output in naturally occurring classroom interaction. *Language Learning*, *62*(3), 851–879. http://dx.doi.org/10.1111/j.1467-9922.2012.00716.x

Hammersley, M. (1998). *Reading Ethnographic Research: A Critical Guide*. London: Longman.

Hopkins, D. (2002). *A Teacher's Guide to Classroom Research*. Maidenhead: Open University Press.

Masson, M. (2011). Collecting student perceptions of feedback through interviews. PAAL 2011 Conference Proceedings. Hong Kong, China.

McKay, S. (2006). *Research Second Language Classrooms*. Mahwah, NJ: Lawrence Erlbaum Associates.

Nunan, D., & Bailey, K. (2009). *Exploring Second Language Classroom Research: A Comprehensive Guide*. Boston, MA: Heinle Cengage Learning.

Spada, N. (1986). The interaction between type of contact and type of instruction: Some effects on the L2 proficiency of adult learners. *Studies in Second Language Acquisition*, *8*(02), 181–199. http://dx.doi.org/10.1017/S0272263100006070

Spada, N., & Lyster, R. (1997). Macroscopic and microscopic views of L2 classrooms. *TESOL Quarterly*, *31*(4), 787–792. http://dx.doi.org/10.2307/3587763

Ullmann, R., & Geva, E. (1982). *The Target Language Observation Scheme (TALOS). New York Board of Education, Core French Evaluation Project*. Toronto: Ontario Institute for Studies in Education.

Wajnryb, R. (1993). *Classroom Observation Tasks: A Resource Book for Language Teachers and Trainers*. Cambridge: Cambridge University Press.

6 Case Study Research Framework

Chapter Preview

In this chapter the basic concept and components of a case study research framework will be presented. What is a case study? Why do we choose a case study framework? What are the characteristics? How do we conduct a case study? These are some of the key questions addressed in this chapter. Key procedures to collect and analyze data within a case study research framework will be discussed. The advantages and disadvantages of using this framework will be explored. An exemplary case study will be presented to show and to describe to readers how such a study is conducted and how findings are presented. Key terms associated with case study research and sources for further reading will be provided at the end of the chapter.

6.1 What Are the Key Concepts and Components?

Nunan and Bailey (2009: 158) have defined a case study as "a detailed, often longitudinal investigation of a single individual or entity or a few individuals or entities." A case study is an intensive empirical enquiry that investigates a contemporary phenomenon within its real-life context. It can be longitudinal, as it sometimes spreads over a long period of time. A researcher observes the characteristics of an individual or a unit (a class or school, for example), with the intent of making generalizations about the wider population to which the unit belongs. The case study is considered a naturalistic and qualitative research framework with no manipulation of subjects, and no specific treatment.

Duff (2008: 32–33) argues that the individual case study "... is usually selected for study on the basis of specific psychological, biological, sociocultural, institutional or linguistic attributes, representing a particular age group, a combination of first and second language ability level (e.g. basic or advanced), or a skill area such as writing, a linguistic domain such as morphology and syntax, or mode or medium of learning, such as an online, computer-mediated environment".

A case study is not a standard methodological package like an observational study or an experimental study. It is rather an instance in action, and the researcher investigates the way that his instance functions in a specific context. A case study normally considers data from different sources, examines an issue/problem in real life and uses theory to generalize the main findings. Key components in a case study are: research questions; proposition(s); analysis; linking of data to proposition(s); and criteria for interpreting the main findings.

In a case study questions are raised about a specific object (proposition) which needs to be studied in the case. The unit of analysis can be an individual or a unit (a group of students, a school, etc.). Data collection instruments normally include questionnaires and interviews, but in a case study the researcher can use multiple procedures (both qualitative and quantitative). The data analysis is linked to the case the researcher is trying to demonstrate and/or prove.

Several authors (Nunan 1992; Hamel 1993; Johnson 1993) have identified a number of practical steps the researcher needs to consider if they intend to embark on research using a case study framework:

1. the researcher should define the object of study before the study begins;
2. the researcher should select the case study and ground his/her case on a clear theoretical background;
3. the researcher should decide on the data collection procedures to use;
4. the researcher should provide an interpretation of the data collected and analyzed;
5. the researcher should develop an explanation of the findings;
6. the researches should aim at generalizing the findings.

A case study is a rigorous methodological framework based on a number of criteria (Johnson 1993: 8). It should:

- include a flexible working design;
- make use of multiple data procedures (triangulation);
- include a collection of adequate amounts of data over a period of time;
- ensure validity and credibility of the information;

- present the data collection and analysis procedures in detail;
- attempt to generalize its findings (identify broader implications).

6.2 What Are the Key Data Collection and Analysis Procedures?

A case study normally use data collection instruments such as questionnaires and interviews. However, it is also mistaken to associate a particular data collection procedure to a specific methodological framework in second language research. Case studies, as other research frameworks, use multiple collection procedures, which includes tests, for example. In this section questionnaires and interviews as key data collection for case studies will be presented.

6.2.1 Questionnaires

Questionnaires are very popular instruments for data collection in second language research as they are quite easy to construct. They can be in paper (paper-and-pencil questionnaire) or computer-based format (online, email or telephone), and are very useful tools to ask participants for their opinions and views about language learning and teaching issues. Brown (2001: 6) defines a questionnaire as "... any written instruments that present respondents with a series of questions or statements to which they are to react either by writing out their answers or selecting from among existing answers". A questionnaire measures factual (subject descriptions, demographic characteristics such as age and gender), behavioural (personal history, habits and other characteristics) and attitudinal (opinions, beliefs, attitudes towards particular issues, etc.) data (Dörnyei 2010). There are a number of procedures which need to be taken when developing a questionnaire: deciding on length and format; writing and sequencing the items; and writing appropriate instruction and if necessary translating it into the target language.

Questionnaires are constructed from three possible parts: demographics; closed-ended items and/or open-ended items. The first part includes information and instruction about the questionnaire (instruction, date, etc.) and the respondents (personal information about the questionnaire taker).

The second part of the questionnaire usually includes closed items and/or open items depending on the nature of the questionnaire and the

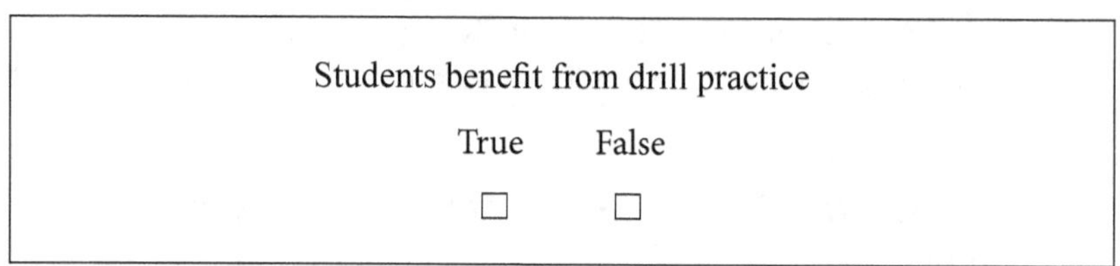

Figure 6.1 Example of closed-ended item (True and False)

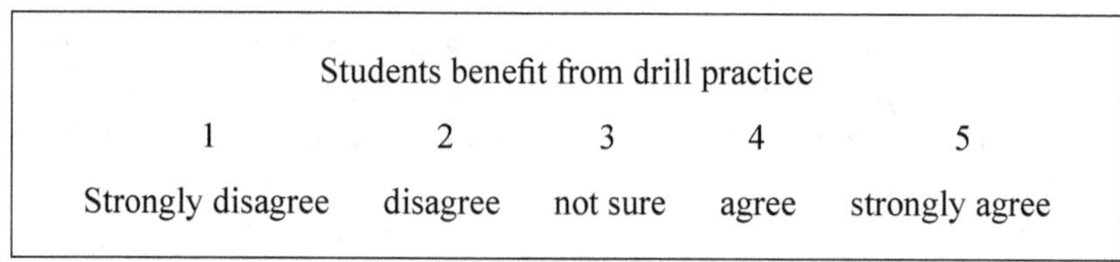

Figure 6.2 Example of a closed-ended item (Likert scale)

information the researcher needs to gather. A closed-ended items questionnaire provides takers with a limited choice (e.g. yes or no, true or false, choose between two options (see Figure 6.1), circle an option that has a numerical value). One typical example is the use of the Likert scale to score a questionnaire. In Figure 6.2 a statement is evaluated by using a 1–5 scale to rate the answers: *strongly disagree*, *disagree*, *not sure*, *agree* and *strongly agree*. Questionnaire takers are asked to circle the number associated with their opinions.

Closed-ended questionnaires can be analyzed using percentages (e.g. how many respondents think that the statement is true) or descriptive statistics (numerical data from a Likert scale for example, usually on a 1–5 scale). Scales can quantify the data in a closed-ended questionnaire. Numerical data can be analyzed statistically to show means and standard deviation, for example.

An open-ended items questionnaire is constructed to request opinions and views from respondents. Examples of open-ended items are short answers and sentence completion items (see the example in Figure 6.3). Data from open-ended questionnaires are qualitative in nature (words). The following analysis procedure is used: the first step is for the researcher to transcribe the data into a separate document; the second step is to decide how the data are recorded and grouped depending on the objectives of the investigation; the third step is to read the information collected and grouped looking for key patterns, reoccurring themes, issues; the final step is the

In what ways do you think students benefit from grammar drill practice? Write your answer below.

Figure 6.3 Open-ended item (short answer item)

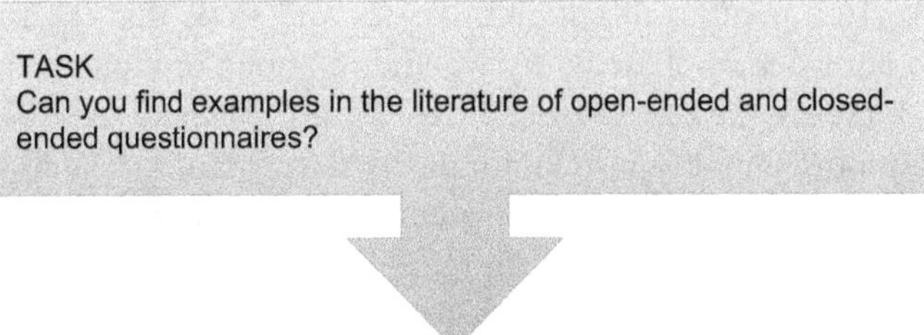

Figure 6.4 Task

interpretation of the questionnaire finding. For each group, the researcher identifies a response and main outcome.

In order to make a questionnaires, whether open-ended or closed-ended, the researcher should consider a number of issues to define the construct and develop the instrument. First of all, the researcher must define the main topic/construct under investigation. The purpose of the questionnaire should be established before the questionnaire is developed. Second, the researcher reviews studies which have used questionnaires to measure the same topic/construct. This will provide the researcher with a possible path to follow. Third, the researcher must work on the practical requirements related to the development of a questionnaire, which include the type and the number of items to be included.

6.2.2 Interviews

Interviews are a useful data collection tools to capture beliefs, opinions, views and reflections from both learners and teachers. The format of an interview depends on a number of factors: the nature and purpose of the study;

practice in previous research; and practical issues such as the time available. In an interview there is an interviewer (usually the researcher) and somebody being interviewed (the interviewee or respondent). Data are gathered through a number of questions previously prepared by the interviewer. There are two types of interviews: open interviews and closed interviews. An open interview question ('What do you think of the communicative language teaching approach?') allows the respondent to provide a broad answer, and it allows the interviewer to ask follow-up questions. Researcher often use open interviews when they need to confirm hypotheses which have been formulated as part of the study they have undertaken. A closed interview is more structured, developed to collect specific information. All the respondents are asked the same questions, in a particular predetermined order.

There are a number of common issues and steps that the researcher needs to consider when deciding whether an open or a closed interview is used. First of all, the researcher must establish what type of interview would be more suitable in relation to the purpose of the study. Second, the population to interview must be identified. The size of the population is also a factor to consider. Third, the questions to be used must be formulated. The researcher can ask a variety of questions: personal questions related to the respondent's previous experience (e.g. proficiency level, scores on a test, etc.); opinions and views about a specific topic or issue; questions about the respondent's feelings; questions to investigate the respondent's knowledge about an issues, theory, research, etc.; or background questions to collect data related to the respondent age, gender, previous job, address, nationality, proficiency level on languages, etc.). Finally, decisions must be made about the length, place and how the data should be collected (e.g. recording, taking notes, written records, etc.).

Once the data have been collected, appropriate procedures for data analysis must be used (see the summary of steps to be taken in Figure 6.6). Analyzing an interview could be a demanding task, as the interview data are mainly words and they must be interpreted to provide meaningful data. First of all, the interviewer needs to become familiar with the data by going over the notes many times, listening to recordings repeatedly, and reading answers over and over again very carefully. The interviewer/researcher develops a series of categories from the data which captures the main meanings of the data itself. One approach is to extrapolate these categories from the data (coding the data). As the researcher analyzes the data very closely and carefully, he/she becomes very familiar with

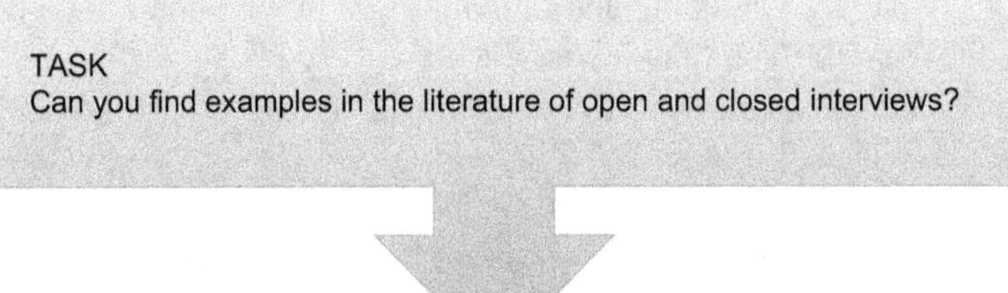

Figure 6.5 Task

Step one: Listening to the recording and transcribing the interview.

Step two: Reading the transcripts carefully.

Step three: Coding the interview: identifying themes and assigning codes.

Step four: Applying the codes consistently throughout the interview transcript.

Step five: Writing a summary of the themes coded from the interview.

Figure 6.6 Steps for interviews analysis

its content. Categories emerge from the data as the interviewer notices similar patterns in the respondents' answers. He/she is able to code the data by identifying specific themes and assigning a short word or phrase for each of them. The researcher does not analyze the data with predetermined categories but identifies categories by reflecting on and interpreting the available data.

Another approach consists of establishing the themes and categories before the interview takes place. The researcher might have formulated specific questions and/or hypotheses and he/she may be in a position to have categories which have been chosen prior to the study.

6.2.3 Introspection Data Instruments

Introspection is another collection data instrument based on the observation and reporting on one individual thought, feeling, reasoning process and mental state. Introspection can occur with an event being reported as it is happening ('What are you doing and thinking right now?') and after a certain period ('What did you think about the activity you have performed?'). This refers to immediate introspective and delayed retrospective think-aloud protocols.

Think-aloud protocols and stimulated recall are two popular verbal report techniques used in second language research. In a think-aloud protocol, the subject is asked to verbalize his/her thoughts during a performance. The researcher's role is to stimulate the verbalization by encouraging the participant to think-aloud about his/her thoughts and feelings. An example of the use of this technique comes from Wesche and Paribakht's study (2000). In this study, the participants were trained in think-aloud procedures. Each participant was asked to look at a picture and describe what he/she was thinking about it while looking at the picture. Following the training, they were asked to perform a series of vocabulary tasks while verbalizing what they were thinking or doing. In this study both immediate introspective and delayed retrospective protocols were used. The data were tape-recorded and the introspections and retrospections transcribed. The analysis of the transcripts consisted of reading the transcripts and identifying the main elements in subjects' responses to each activity. It also involved identifying evidence of subjects' learning and knowledge of lexical items. Reading and analysis was followed by further analysis and discussion to identify common patterns and variations with respect to the research issues and questions.

The simulated recall technique is used by a researcher to prompt a learner to recall and report thoughts that he/she might have while performing a task. The main purpose is to explore participants' thoughts, processes and internal strategies during an event. The event is video-recorded and re-presented to the participants some time later to explore their views about what was going through their minds at the time of the event. This is a key aspect of this technique as it helps to activate participants' memory structures.

6.2.4 Surveys

Survey research in the form of a questionnaire (see Section 6.2.1) is a very common instrument to collect data in second language research. Surveys allow the researcher to investigate a construct by asking questions or opinions. Surveys are instruments used to establish a relationship between a sample and the population from which the sample is drawn. In a survey, the researcher must decide what they are planning to investigate (constructs, concepts, theory, issues, etc.), who will be surveyed (students, language assistants, teachers, etc.), how the population will be sampled (randomly or subjects selected by the teachers), and how many respondents should participate. The larger the better, as the larger the sample is, the more it is representative of the overall population. Just as with questionnaires in some cases, surveys can use quantitative data procedures such as statistical techniques to analyze data.

6.3 What Are the Key Advantages and Disadvantages?

One of the key advantages of using a case study for a small-case research project is that the individual, class or unit the researcher decides to select are ready-made. The natural nature of the study makes this research framework strong in reality. Researchers observe and study a phenomena in a real context from both a process and product perspective. It is a reasonable alternative to an experimental study when populations and other crucial elements of the study cannot be manipulated. Case studies are very useful for studying educational innovations, programme evaluations and to conduct research which might have an impact on educational policy.

Despite the clear advantages to the use of this framework, the use of a single case cannot be considered representative of the phenomena/issue under investigation. In addition, the analysis and interpretation of the data might not be rigorous because of possible subjective bias from the researcher. Finally, there is the question of reliability and validity: Are the findings generalizable?

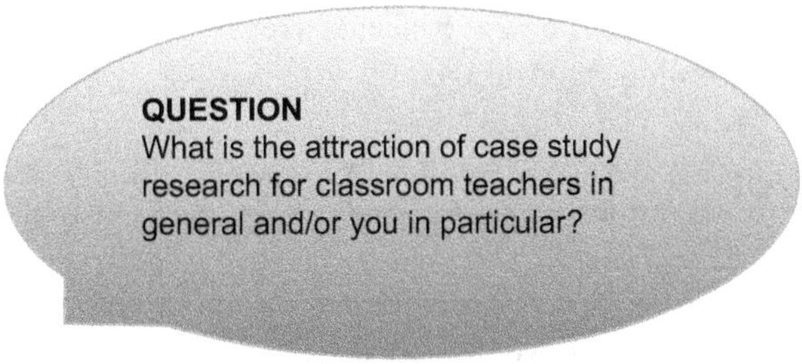

QUESTION
What is the attraction of case study research for classroom teachers in general and/or you in particular?

Figure 6.7 Question

6.4 What Does a Case Study Look Like?

In this section an exemplary case study-based study is presented (Farrell and Choo 2005). The intent is to show how a case study is carried out and describe the different components of this research methodological framework. The title of the study is: "Conceptions of grammar teaching: A case study of teachers' beliefs and classroom practices" (Farrell and Choo 2005).

Purpose of the Study

The study reported in this section is a study investigating the beliefs and practices of two experienced English primary school teachers in relation to teaching grammar in Singapore. The author makes the case for the need to conduct this case study by stating that there is no previous research in this area in relation to practices in primary schools in Singapore.

Research Questions

The study was informed by two main broad questions:

1. What are the two teachers' beliefs about the way grammar should be taught in primary school?
2. What are their actual classroom practices of teaching grammar?

The researcher also intended to address the question of how the beliefs corresponded to the observed classroom practice and any other possible factors affecting the two teachers in terms of their grammar teaching practices. The two teachers of this case study were both very experienced English language teachers.

Design and Procedures

The researcher adopted a case study methodological framework to investigate the two questions. Data were collected over a period of two months and consisted of the following instruments:

- a pre-study interview with the two teachers (this was piloted);
- two observations of the teachers' classes (audio recording and field notes);
- pre- and post-class interviews; and
- random samples of students' written work.

The interview questions were specifically developed and designed to elicit information in two distinct areas: gathering information about the teachers' beliefs regarding grammar, grammar teaching and grammar corrections; and obtaining information about the teachers' teaching practices and what factors might have influenced their approaches and strategies.

The interviews were the key instrument in collecting information about teachers' beliefs. The interviews lasted one hour each. They were audio-recorded, transcribed and coded to be fully analyzed. Each of the two teachers was preliminarily interviewed (a pre-study interview was used) to collect information about their experience. Following this interview a pre-lesson and post-interview approach was used to gather information about the lesson plan and help the teachers reflect on their teaching.

Two classroom non-participatory observations were conducted over a period of two months. The researcher obtained information about each teacher's teaching practices through the use of audio recordings and field notes from the lesson observations. Both the field notes and the audio recordings were transcribed. This information was used by the observer/researcher to engage in discussion with the teacher about their practices. The lesson plans, instructional materials and random samples of students' marked composition scripts were also collected and used for analysis.

Results and Interpretation

Two set of results were obtained from the case study: one regarding the teachers' beliefs, and one regarding the teachers' practices. The following main findings were obtained in each set.

Beliefs

These are the main findings about the two teachers' beliefs about the way grammar should be taught in primary school:

- The teaching of grammar is a crucial factor in improving learners' ability to produce accurate and correct written work.
- Learners don't necessarily need to be able to explain grammar rules explicitly, but they need to be able to apply rules and grammatical structures correctly in sentences. This is paramount if we want to avoid errors in learners' speech and in writing.
- The use of drill practice is beneficial for learners. One of the teachers expressed a distinct preference for the use of explicit teaching of grammar rules and sentence structures, and the utilization of drills and paradigms in grammar teaching. The other one preferred a mixed approach to grammar teaching where both explicit explanation of rules followed by mechanical practice and more communicative approaches can coexist.

- One of the teachers believed that there is place for incidental teaching of grammar (inductive grammar approaches), considering that learners might not have the necessary language skills to benefit from it.
- Both teachers provided similar feedback on their students' compositions. They marked each grammar error and provided the correct version on the written composition.

Overall, both teachers adopted a traditional approach to grammar teaching. The observed lessons indicated that the teaching approach was teacher-centred, with both teachers providing explanations and instructions, and asking questions and eliciting responses from the students on their knowledge of grammar items. However, one of the two teachers was trying, from time to time, to integrate grammar learning and teaching into other language skills activities.

Beliefs and Classroom Practices

The findings indicated that the two teachers had slightly different beliefs and classroom practices in terms of grammar teaching. For one teacher there was a clear convergence between beliefs (partly influenced by their own learning and teaching experience) and actual classroom practices. This teacher believed that learners can benefit from an explicit, deductive and traditional approach to grammar teaching. The classroom practices of this teacher reflected this belief. For the other teacher, however, there was less convergence between beliefs and actual practices. The teacher expressed the belief that grammar teaching should be integrated into the practice of other language skills such as speaking, writing and reading. However, the classroom practices of this teacher were mixed, using only a few activities where grammar practice was contextualized into meaningful communicative situations. Most of the grammar was explicitly taught and the grammar practice was mainly structured and prescriptive.

Discussion and Conclusion

This case study investigated the beliefs and instructional practices of two experienced teachers of English language in a primary school in Singapore. The main findings of this study suggest that teachers have a set of beliefs that are sometimes not reflected in their classroom practices. There are a number of reasons which explain this divergence:

1. Time seems to be a constraint for both teachers. They both argued that most of their classroom instructional decisions were directly

influenced by the syllabus and the lack of time. Therefore the deductive approach to grammar teaching seemed more appropriate as it required less time for preparation. They both argued that they had no control of the syllabus and their classroom practices were influenced by schools' and parents' demands and expectations.

2. Teachers' reverence for traditional grammar instruction was another key factor. Both teachers expressed some enthusiasm for deductive approaches of grammar teaching. However, they continued to employ a traditional approach to grammar teaching as they believed that traditional grammar teaching would result in more accurate use of the target language.

Even though generalizations of this case study are very problematic, one of the main contributions of this study is the opportunity given to the teachers to reflect on their beliefs and practices in the language classroom. Language teachers may learn much about the importance of accessing teachers' beliefs and comparing these beliefs with actual classroom practices.

TASK

Find the following article: Otha, A. (1995). Applying sociocultural theory to analysis of learner discourse: Collaborative interaction in the zone of proximal development. *Issues in Applied Linguistics*, *6*(2), 93–121. Read it and answer the following questions:

1. Can you describe the case?
2. Describe the question or questions the author was trying to answer.
3. Describe the design.
4. Present the results. Were you convinced? Do you accept the conclusions of the author or authors?

Figure 6.8 Task

6.5 What Are the Key Terms?

Case stands for the unit of investigation for case study design research. A case can be one object or one person, or it can be a group of persons. A case is anything that can be investigated that can be clearly defined and identified.

Longitudinal is related to the word *long*. A research investigation is longitudinal if data are collected over a period of time or gathered multiple times. The opposite of longitudinal is *cross-sectional*. Cross-sectional research means data are gathered at one time only. Case studies tend to be longitudinal.

Naturalistic refers to something occurring in an ordinary or usual way, and not studied in isolation. In this sense, *naturalistic* is the opposite of *experimental*. Naturalistic inquiry emphasizes gathering data that renders faithful and authentic accounts by researchers who were present. It is closely associated with participant-observation data collection.

6.6 What Are the Key Readings?

Brown, D. (2001). *Teaching by Principles: An Interactive Approach to Language Pedagogy*. London: Longman.

Brown, J.D., & Rogers, T. S. (2002). *Doing Second Language Research*. Oxford: Oxford University Press.

Casanave, C. (2010). Case studies. In B. Paltridge, & A. Phakti (Eds.). *Continuum Companion to Research Methods in Applied Linguistics* (pp. 66–79). London: Continuum.

Cohen, L., Manion, L., & Morrison, K. (2000). *Research Methods in Education* (2nd ed.). London: Routledge.

Creswell, J. (2002). *Educational Research: Planning, Conducting, and Evaluating Quantitative and Qualitative Research*. Upper Saddle River, NJ: Merrill Prentice Hall.

Creswell, J. (2003). *Research Design: Qualitative, Quantitative, and Mixed Methods Approaches* (2nd ed.). Thousand Oaks, CA: SAGE.

Dörnyei, Z. (2007). *Research Methods in Applied Linguistics: Quantitative, Qualitative and Mixed Methodologies*. Oxford: Oxford University Press.

Dörnyei, Z. (2010). *Questionnaires in Second Language Research: Construction, Administration, and Processing*. London: Routledge.

Duff, P. (2008). *Case Study Research in Applied Linguistics*. New York, NY: Routledge.

Farrell, T., & Choo, P. (2005). Conceptions of grammar teaching: A case study of teachers' beliefs and classroom practices. *TESL-EJ*, *9*(2), 1–13.

Gass, S., & Mackey, A. (2000). *Stimulated Recall Methodology in Second Language Research*. New York, NY: Routledge.

Hamel, J. (1993). *Case Study Methods*. Thousand Oaks, CA: SAGE.

Johnson, D. (1993). Classroom-oriented research in second language learning. In A. Omaggio-Hadley, & D. Johnson (Eds.), *Research in Language Learning* (pp. 1–23). Lincolnwood, IL: National Textbook Company.

McKay, S. (2006). *Researching Second Language Classrooms*. Mahwah, NJ: Lawrence Erlbaum.

Nunan, D. (1992). *Research Methods in Language Learning*. Cambridge: Cambridge Language Teaching Library.

Nunan, D., & Bailey, K. (2009). *Exploring Second Language Classroom Research: A Comprehensive Guide*. Boston, MA: Heinle Cengage Learning.

Schwandt, T. (2007). *The SAGE Dictionary of Qualitative Inquiry*. Thousand Oaks, CA: SAGE.

Wesche, M., & Paribakht, S. (2000). Reading-based exercises in second language vocabulary learning: An introspective study. *Modern Language Journal*, *84*(2), 196–213. http://dx.doi.org/10.1111/0026-7902.00062

Part Three

Mixed Frameworks and Psycholinguistic Methods

In Part Three, mixed frameworks to second language research will be described (Chapter 7). Psycholinguistic research will be presented (Chapter 7) and a brief and concise summary of the main research components in second language research will be discussed (Chapter 8).

7 Mixed Research Frameworks and Psycholinguistic Methods

Chapter Preview

In this chapter the argument for a process and product component and the use of mixed research frameworks will be considered. Key components will be identified and how we conduct study using this research framework will be discussed.

In the second part of the chapter, psycholinguistic methods to collect and analyze data will be presented. This will include self-paced listening and reading, eye tracking, ERPs, and priming, among others.

7.1 Why and How Is a Mixed Research Framework Used?

In last 50 years, both quantitative and qualitative approaches have been used in second language research. Research in the 1970s and 1980s saw predominance for a quantitative approach with an emphasis on the 'product'. In the 1990s, however, researchers began to develop designs which included a process component and were qualitative in nature. Spada (1987), investigating the possible relation between type of contact and type of instruction in a communicative language teaching context, used both a process and product mixed design. Both qualitative and quantitative data were collected using COLT and language tests.

Quantitative research is defined as an inquiry into a social or human problem based on testing a theory composed of variables, measured with numbers, and analyzed with statistical procedures, in order to determine whether the predictive generalizations of the theory hold true (Creswell 1994).

Qualitative research is, according to Gass and Mackey (2005: 162), "research that is based on descriptive data that does not make (regular) use of statistical procedures."

The use of a mixed research framework is desirable in second language research as it combines the strengths of both a qualitative and quantitative approach to data collection and analysis. Thus, for example, quantitative research has a number of strengths: conceptualization of variables, or measuring and comparing possible relationships between variables using large samples. Qualitative research has different strengths: in-depth study of a small-scale sample and methodological flexibility which help the researcher to investigate process and change.

The quantitative approach conceptualizes the main variables, and studies relationships between them. It rests on measurement, and samples are typically larger than in qualitative studies. Data collection analysis is well developed, and codified methods make it easy to replicate the study. The quantitative approach means that certain types of important questions can be systematically answered.

The qualitative approach deals with cases and it is context- and process-oriented compared to the product-oriented nature of the quantitative approach. Samples are small in qualitative research. It is quite a flexible approach which can be used in a variety of real-life situations, for a wider range of issues and perspectives.

The use of a mixed methodological framework depends on the research questions being addressed by the researcher. The possible combination of the two approaches might offer the valuable opportunity to combine their strengths to increase the scope and depth of a study.

The question is: How do we combine the two approaches? Creswell and Plano Clark (2007: 79–84) have identified three main dimensions: the timing; the mixing; and the weighting. The first relates to the order followed by the researcher in terms of the time and sequence of data collection. The weighting dimension relates to how balanced the approach of the researcher is towards the qualitative and qualitative option: is there equal weighting? The mixing dimension refers to how the two approaches will be mixed: merging both approaches; embedding one within the other; or connecting the two. In the embedded mixed research framework, for example, the researcher needs to collect both qualitative and quantitative data, but one data set plays a secondary role compared to the other set. In the embedded research framework, for example, a researcher uses a secondary qualitative component (interview) in a quantitative experimental study comparing groups' performance, to collect different views from the participants about their learning experience. In a mixed research framework, where both qualitative and quantitative data are connected, qualitative data collection might precede quantitative. This is because it is very common to adopt qualitative instruments to develop a better understanding of certain issues in a study before launching into a quantitative analysis of the phenomenon. Examples would be where the researcher needs to create a testing instrument, but needs a deeper understanding of the phenomenon in question. The choice of using a mixed framework is dictated by the inherent logic of the study undertaken, by the way the research problem is framed and set up for research, and especially by the way its research questions are formulated. Mixed methods research requires specific skills, and the researcher must develop a good background and experience in both quantitative and qualitative research.

An exemplary mixed research framework study is the one conducted by Scott, Kolano and Wang (2010) investigating gender differences in motivation to learn among students of Spanish in a high school in the United States. The study employed a mixed methodology research framework to investigate a possible relationship between gender differences and motivational factors among learners. The researchers collected quantitative data in the form of a questionnaire using a seven-point Likert scale system to quantify learners' responses (seven points for the "strongly agree" option and one point for the "strongly disagree" option). The questionnaire was constructed on the basis of previous attitude motivations tests which gauge learners' motivation to learn another language. The scores were analyzed using *t*-tests to test possible statistical differences between males and females. Qualitative data were also collected by interviewing learners and teachers. The interview questions addressed motivational and attitudinal factors towards learning another language. Each interview lasted for about 30 minutes and was tape-recorded. The data were transcribed and coded, looking for significant and emergent themes during a careful analysis of the data. This inductive approach is based on the so-called 'grounded theory', which emphasizes the importance of extrapolating the main themes from the data rather than having preconceived notions regarding the data. The main findings from this study indicated that the male students perceived themselves to be less motivated than their female peers, but gender differences were less dramatic than in previous studies. The study's results also suggest that males and females have opposing preferences with respect to L2 classroom management.

Another good example of a mixed methodological research framework study was carried out by Sato (2013). In this study the researcher investigated the beliefs of second language learners regarding peer interaction and peer corrective feedback and the possible effects of intervention (designed to promote collaborative learning) in changing those beliefs. The subjects of this study were Japanese native speakers learning English at

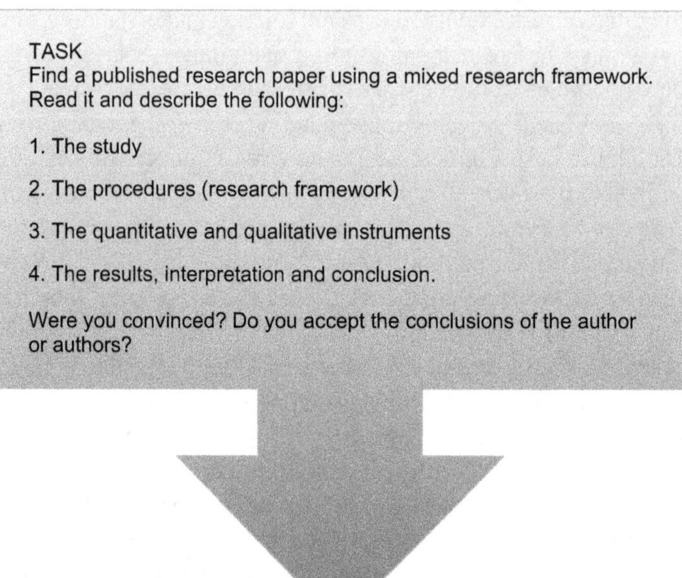

Figure 7.1 Task

university. Groups received different types of interventions: peer interaction instruction; corrective feedback (prompts or recasts); and a control group.

A questionnaire was used before and after the instructional period. It consisted of 27 questions to elicit information from participants about their beliefs regarding classroom format and practice (communicative orientation), opportunities to communicate between learners and the use of corrective feedback. The questionnaire used a Likert-scale system to score the participants' answers and *t*-tests were used to measure beliefs on peer interaction and corrective feedback before and after intervention. An interview was the qualitative data instrument in this study. It was an open-ended interview developed to gather information about learners' view on peer interaction and peer corrective feedback. The interviews were all transcribed and coded on the basis of the grounded theory methodology. Among the coding categories the researcher identified peer interaction and peer corrective feedback. The quantitative (*t*-tests) and qualitative (grounded theory methodology) analyses revealed that learners benefited from the intervention. It had beneficial effects on collaborative learning, language development, and improved collaborative classroom environment and social relationships between learners.

7.2 What Are the Main Psycholinguistic Methods Used in Second Language Research?

The number of studies in second language research employing online research methodology has increased over the years. This is mainly due to the fact that psycholinguistics research and language processing are playing a key role in understanding they way people acquire a second language. As indicated by Roberts (2012), psycholinguistic methods are often mixed with more traditional ones in an attempt to address central issues in second language acquisition, such as assessing L2 knowledge, and real-time processing. Jegerski and VanPatten (2014) provide a good account of the research methods used in psycholinguistics to explore and investigate second language processes and processing. Some of the main psycholinguistic methods used in language research will be described in this chapter.

7.2.1 Self-paced Reading/Listening

Self-paced reading and self-paced listening are both implemented using computerized online software responsible for recording listening and reading time. Learners read a word or a phrase at their own speed. They are asked to push a button to bring up the next word or phrase once they have managed to process the information required. They keep repeating the procedure until they have processed all the input set by the researcher for the experiment. Response to online real-time processing is recorded by the experimental software. In most cases a non-cumulative technique is used. In this technique only one segment (word or phrase) is visible to the learner at a time. When the next one is revealed, the previous one is masked. The self-paced technique provides the researcher with a measure of real-time processing and comprehension. Most studies, using this technique, investigate specific issues in second language acquisition such as violations and ambiguity. It is an effective online method for sentence processing research.

One exemplary study using a self-paced reading task is the one conducted by Jackson (2008) to explore how L2 German speakers at different proficiency levels use case-marking information when processing subject-object ambiguities in German. In this study, learners were exposed to the sentences through a non-cumulative self-paced reading test. They were told to sit in front of a computer and press the spacebar once at a time. Each time they pressed the spacebar they saw a word or sentence appear and the previous word or phrase disappeared. After they read each sentence, participants read a comprehension statement on the screen. They then had to determine

Read the following article: Roberts, L., & Lizska, S. (2013). Processing tense/aspect-agreement violations on-line in the second language: A self-paced reading study with French and German L2 learners of English. *Second Language Research*, *29*(4), 413–439.

Describe the psycholinguistic methods used in this study.

Figure 7.2 Task

whether the statement corresponded to the meaning of the sentence or not and they had to press "correct" or "false". Results from the self-paced test indicated that advanced L2 German speakers rapidly integrated case-marking information during online processing, exhibiting a subject preference similar to German native speakers. However, there was evidence that the relative processing difficulty of object-first sentences was influenced by early access to the thematic verb. In contrast, intermediate L2 speakers were not immediately sensitive to case-marking information, regardless of thematic verb placement.

Another example is the study conducted by De Jong (2005) to examine whether grammar can be learned through listening. Learners involved in this study were divided into three groups receiving different training conditions in which Spanish noun-adjective gender agreement was the learning target. The first group received receptive training; the second group received receptive and productive training; and a third group served as a control. Receptive and productive knowledge were assessed through the use of different tasks, including a self-paced listening test. This online comprehension measure was used, requiring responses from learners while the input was still being processed. The self-placed listening task was developed to measure the speed of input processing. The participants pressed a key to hear the next words of the sentence. Each sentence was split into five phrases, and each phrase was spoken with an intonation as if it were part of a sentence. Participants were asked to go through each sentence as quickly as possible and to indicate whether the sentence and picture matched by pressing a button. Results suggest that the receptive and receptive/productive training programmes succeeded in building a knowledge base that was used in comprehension but much less so in production.

7.2.2 Cross-modal Priming

Cross-modal priming is an effective method to investigate moment-by-moment sentence comprehension. Learners are asked to process the input and make a response (choose a binary option, name a picture or word, etc.) as quickly as possible to a target stimulus. The stimulus is presented on a screen and comparisons are made in response times between target and non-target stimuli. Faster response times reflect greater activation levels, thus the researcher can examine what linguistic items are more or less activated in the learner's mind. Psycholinguistic studies often employ priming paradigms to address issues of whether and when certain representations are active in the course of language processing. In priming studies, researchers typically examine changes compared to a baseline level of performance in responding to a 'target' stimulus when the target is preceded by a 'prime' stimulus. This method is very natural as it allows for the stimulus materials to be presented uninterrupted and at a normal speech rate. It is used for studies related to lexical and grammatical online processing.

Felser and Roberts, for example, (2007) investigated the real-time processing of *wh*-dependencies by advanced Greek-speaking learners of English using a cross-modal picture-priming task. Participants were asked to respond to different types of picture targets presented while listening to sentences containing indirect-object relative clauses. The sentences were read with natural intonation, and pre-recorded on a digital tape recorder. Pictures of animals and inanimate objects were used as visual targets. For each experimental sentence two visual targets were selected: an 'identical' picture target showing the referent of the indirect object noun; and a picture showing an unrelated object. Each participant was tested individually in an experimental laboratory. They were seated in front of a computer and asked to listen carefully to the pre-recorded sentences over headphones, and to watch the screen for pictures that would appear at some point during each sentence. The participants were told that whenever a picture appeared on the screen they had to decide as quickly as possible whether the animal or object in the picture was alive or not alive, by pushing either the left or the right-hand button of a dual push-button box. Participants' response times were measured from the point at which the picture appeared on the screen to their pressing one of the response buttons.

7.2.3 Eye-tracking with Text

Eye-tracking is a method used to monitor, examine and record learners' visual attention, visual search and language processing during spoken or reading language processing. Eye-tracking is a method used to inform researchers with regard to eye movement behaviours. For example, it records where and for how long a participant is looking at an element in a sentence and/or where his/her eyes move next. As Keating (2014: 71) has pointed out, the movement of the eyes across a sentence is not a straight line from left to right, it "... is much more turbulent. The eyes move in a series of jumps called *saccades*. Saccades are separated by short periods during which the eyes remain relatively still, called *fixations*." During reading, saccades move the eyes across the text in order to process particular words. Participants then spend most of the time, when reading a text, in fixations. This method is useful for detecting readers' sensitivity to ungrammaticalities, the interpretation of ambiguous grammatical features, and for investigating online parsing procedures. This method gives researchers the opportunity to examine the moment-by-moment comprehension processes in a more natural way than, for instance, self-paced reading. Furthermore, it provides and records a more fine-grained reading profile of the different processing stages in reading: the so-called 'first fixations', which is the first time the eyes fixate on the region of interest (e.g. a particular word, sentence segments, etc.); the 'first-pass' times, which sums up the time spent reading the region of interest from the first fixation until the eyes exit to the right or to the left; and how often the word was returned to for re-reading (regressions).

Eye tracking is a novel and valuable methodological procedure in second language acquisition research, which has been employed for different purposes (Frenck-Mestre, 2005). Some eye-tracking studies have looked into syntactic ambiguity resolution by bilinguals (Roberts, Gullberg and Indefrey 2008) to investigate the influence of the L1 on L2 processing. Eye tracking has also been used to measure 'noticing' (Schmidt, 1995) of new forms in written L2 input. Keating (2009) investigated the eye movements of native Spanish speakers and English-speaking learners of Spanish as they read a number of sentences that contained nouns modified by post-nominal adjectives located in three different syntactic domains. The results indicate that gender agreement is acquirable in adulthood, and that the distance that separates nouns and adjectives affects the detection of gender anomalies in the second language.

7.2.4 Event-related Potentials (ERPs)

ERPs research is a method used for exploring human cognitive language processing. ERPs reflect the real-time electrophysiological brain activity of cognitive processes that are time-locked to the presentation of target stimuli (Morgan-Short and Tanner, 2014). Language-related ERPs research often employs a violation paradigm for presenting linguistic stimuli. In this paradigm, the ERPs response to a linguistic violation (e.g. lexical, syntactic, morphosyntactic) is compared to the ERPs response to a matched control word or structure. As argued by Morgan-Short and Tanner (2014), ERPs data provides data related to timing effects (responses to a stimulus), effect polarity (positive or negative wave from a manipulation) and scalp distribution (making use of electrodes across the scalp). Various types of violation (also called difficulties, disruptions, anomalies, etc.) have been shown to elicit particular ERP components in the L1. The ERPs technique allows the researcher to take the electrical activity recorded from the brain, and use it to investigate cognitive processing. Researchers can record participants while they perform a task designed to elicit the proper cognitive response (e.g. attending to a specific linguistics property). To accomplish this, participants are asked to wear a mesh cap embedded with electrodes which record brain activity. In addition, electrodes can be used in the face to monitor eye movements. An example of a study where the researchers used this technique is Steinhauer, White, and Drury (2009), where it was investigated whether age of acquisition may affect morphosyntax in second language acquisition. ERPs were used to measure online possible effects. The study revealed that there is little evidence for the critical period hypothesis in the domain of late-acquired second language morphosyntax. Instead, proficiency seems to be a critical factor in predicting brain activity patterns in second language processing.

7.3 What Are the Key Readings?

Creswell, J. (1994). *Research Design: Qualitative and Quantitative Approaches.* Thousand Oaks, CA: SAGE.

Creswell, J. (2008). *Educational Research: Planning, Conducting and Evaluating Quantitative and Qualitative Research* (3rd ed.). Upper Saddle River, NJ: Pearson.

Creswell, J., & Plano Clark, L. (2007). *Designing and Conducting Mixed Methods Research.* Thousand Oaks, CA: SAGE.

De Jong, N. (2005). Can second language grammar be learned through listening? An experimental study. *Studies in Second Language Acquisition*, *27*, 205–234. http://dx.doi.org/10.1017/S0272263105050114

Felser, C., & Roberts, L. (2007). Processing *wh*-dependencies in a second language: A cross-modal priming study. *Second Language Research*, *23*(1), 9–36. http://dx.doi.org/10.1177/0267658307071600

Frenck-Mestre, C. (2005). Eye-movement recording as a tool for studying syntactic processing in a second language: A review of methodologies and experimental findings. *Second Language Research*, *21*(2), 175–198. http://dx.doi.org/10.1191/0267658305sr257oa

Jackson, C. (2008). Proficiency level and the interaction of lexical and morphosyntactic information during L2 sentence processing. *Language Learning*, *58*(4), 875–909. http://dx.doi.org/10.1111/j.1467-9922.2008.00481.x

Jegerski, J., & VanPatten, B. (Eds.). (2014). *Research Methods in Second Language Psycholinguistics*. New York, NY: Routledge.

Keating, G. (2009). Sensitivity to violations in gender agreement in native and non-native Spanish: An eye-movement investigation. *Language Learning*, *59*(3), 503–535. http://dx.doi.org/10.1111/j.1467-9922.2009.00516.x

Keating, G. (2014). Eye-tracking with text. In J. Jegerski, & B. VanPatten (Eds.), *Research Methods in Second Language Psycholinguistics*, (pp. 69–92). New York, NY: Routledge.

Marinis, T. (2003). Psycholinguistic techniques in second language acquisition research. *Second Language Research*, *19*(2), 144–161. http://dx.doi.org/10.1191/0267658303sr217ra

Morgan-Short, K., & Tanner, D. (2014). Event-related potentials (ERPs). In J. Jegerski, & B. VanPatten (Eds.), *Research Methods in Second Language Psycholinguistics*, (pp. 127–152). New York, NY: Routledge.

Plano Clark, L., & Creswell, J. (2008). *The Mixed Methods Reader*. Thousand Oaks, CA: SAGE.

Roberts, L. (2012). Psycholinguistic techniques and resources in second language acquisition research. *Second Language Research*, *28*(1), 113–127. http://dx.doi.org/10.1177/0267658311418416

Roberts, L., & Lizska, S.A. (2013). Processing tense/aspect-agreement violations on-line in the second language: A self-paced reading study with French and German L2 learners of English. *Second Language Research*, *29*(4), 413–439. http://dx.doi.org/10.1177/0267658313503171

Roberts, L., Gullberg, M., & Indefrey, P. (2008). Online pronoun resolution in L2 discourse: L1 influence and general learner effects. *Studies in Second Language Acquisition*, *30*(03), 333–357. http://dx.doi.org/10.1017/S0272263108080480

Sato, M. (2013). Beliefs about peer interaction and peer corrective feedback: Efficacy of classroom intervention. *Modern Language Journal*, *97*(3), 611–633. http://dx.doi.org/10.1111/j.1540-4781.2013.12035.x

Schmidt, R. (1995). Consciousness and foreign language learning: A tutorial on the role of attention and awareness in learning. In R. Schmidt (Ed.), *Attention and Awareness in Foreign Language Learning*, (pp. 1–64). Honolulu: University of Hawai'i.

Scott, K., Kolano, Q., & Wang C. (2010). Perceptions of gender differences in high school students' motivation to learn Spanish. *Foreign Language Annals*, *43*(2), 703–721.

Spada, N. (1987). Relationships between instructional differences and learning outcomes: A process–product study of communicative language teaching. *Applied Linguistics*, *8*(2), 137–161. http://dx.doi.org/10.1093/applin/8.2.137

Steinhauer, K., White, E., & Drury, J. (2009). Temporal dynamics of late second language acquisition: Evidence from event-related brain potentials. *Second Language Research*, *25*(1), 13–41. http://dx.doi.org/10.1177/0267658308098995

8 Research Components in a Nutshell

Chapter Preview

In this book the reader has been provided with an overall view of how research in second language learning and teaching is conducted using different research frameworks such as action research, experimental designs, observations, case studies and psycholinguistic methods. The main principles and components of these frameworks have been explored and an exemplary study for each of them provided. Instruments to collect and analyze data were presented from both a qualitative, quantitative and mixed perspective. In the following sections some of the most common questions in relation to second language research will be considered.

8.1 How Do You Develop an Idea for a Study?

Research is a "systematic process of inquiry consisting of three elements or components: (1) a question, problem or hypothesis, (2) data, and (3) analysis and interpretation." (Nunan 1992: 3). Developing a question, problem or hypothesis involves developing a good idea! We should never assume that, if we notice that two things usually happen together, there is a clear relationship between them. This is not always the case, as an observable phenomenon is the result of other factors which might have not been considered. Good ideas can certainly generate from intuitions and observations but at the same time must be grounded in theory and empirical research. You can develop an interest for a topic such as "the role of grammar teaching in second language learning". Through your reading and review of the relevant literature (theory and empirical evidence) you manage to focus your original interest/idea (research area) and narrow down the topic of your study (see example in Figure 8.1) to formulate researchable questions.

Good and researchable ideas come from a number of sources and activities. Reading published and unpublished material will help you to establish what we do and do not know about a phenomenon, a theory and/or the key issue. It will help you to identify a gap in the existing knowledge (one

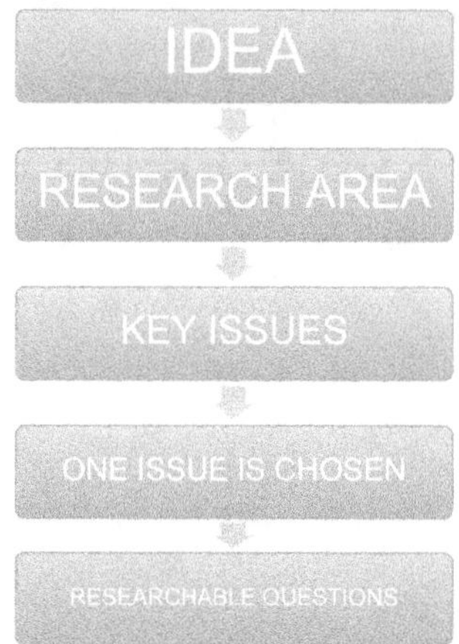

Figure 8.1 Narrowing-down process from the original idea to the questions of the study

issue is chosen). It will help you to make a case: *Why* at this point in time I am the one who is going to embark in this research? Talking to people and experts will help to clarify issues, identifying gaps in the knowledge and evaluating what is already taking place. Attending conferences will help you to discover the direction of new developments and find out what is actually going on. In your journey to develop an idea for a study, you need to clarify *what* specific aspects of a particular field are of most concern to you. You need to think about what the purpose of your investigation might be, about why you are interested in finding out more about the issue. This process will help you identify a list of priorities and then decide what is the most important.

8.2 How Do You Formulate Research Questions?

Very often, whatever the question a researcher comes to formulate, it is possible that the topic proposed has been addressed by other researchers before. This is actually very good news! Creating a research question is a considerable task. You start with what interests you, and you gradually refine the question until it is important and workable.

Here are some good tips about what a good question should look like: it should be relevant, manageable, clear, simple and interesting. The question will be of academic, intellectual interest and relevance to your peers in the field. Questions arise from issues raised in the literature review. The first step in any investigation is to find out what other people have discovered about the topic. The literature review will provide you with the platform to discuss and cite the relevant published material. It is an opportunity to show the reader how you have managed to critically analyze what you have read. The literature review is the theoretical background underpinning your study. It provides the motivation for the study and leads to the main questions you are planning to investigate. There is a strong connection between the review/analysis of what other researchers have done and discovered about the questions in your study. The reader must be able to read the literature review and almost be in the position to anticipate the research questions you are planning to address. The questions set out what you hope to learn about the topic. The question, together with your methodological framework, will guide the choice of data collection and analysis. Some research questions focus your attention onto the relationship of particular theories and constructs: Does this theory/construct/approach effect the acquisition of English morphology? Other research questions aim to open an area to let possible new theories emerge: What is going on here?

You should be able to establish a clear purpose for your research in relation to the chosen field, such as filling a gap in the existing theories, analyzing teaching practices, comparing different approaches or testing theories within a specific population's characteristics (age, gender, background, first language, motivation, etc.).

You need to be realistic about the main purpose and scale of the study you are proposing to undertake. Are you in a position to access the population? Do you have the specific tools to collect the data you need to fully address your questions? Are you able to access this data within the limited time and resources you have available to you?

You need to work out how you can gain access to the resources and tools you need to complete the study. Complex and unclear questions can sometimes lead to a confused research process. Questions have to be clear and simple! The question also needs to intrigue you and maintain your passion throughout your study. Make sure that you have a grounded and motivated interest in your research questions!

8.3 How Do You Write a Literature Review?

The literature review is difficult to write! It is easy to write a summary (a descriptive account of what other researchers have said and done), but it is quite a challenge to produce a critical and analytical account of what they have said and done about a specific topic. The literature review is an in-depth synthesis of what (main purpose of the study) and how (methodological research framework) has been done in a particular field of research. In order to successfully review the relevant literature about a specific topic you need to apply certain categories to act as a filter in your reading. Each study

Table 8.1 Key points for literature review analysis

Author date	*Topic questions*	*Theoretical model*	*Methodological framework*	*Context and setting*	*Findings*	*Limitations and gaps*

TASK

Read the two studies below and answer the following questions:

Benati, A. (2005). The effects of processing instruction, traditional instruction and meaning–output instruction on the acquisition of English simple past tense. *Language Teaching Research* 9(1), 67–93.

Farley, A. (2004). The relative effects of processing instruction and meaning-based output instruction. In B. VanPatten (Ed.), *Processing Instruction: Theory, Research, and Commentary*, (pp. 143–168). Mahwah, NJ: Erlbaum.

1. What are the main findings? Are they different?
2. Do the authors have contrasting views?
3. What is/are the next step/s for further research?

Figure 8.2 Task

you review (e.g. paper, article, chapter in book, research account, etc.) must be analyzed in terms of certain categories: motivation; research framework; what the results say and do not say; and the significance and limitations of the study. You should then provide a synthesis of each category across the relevant studies reviewed. This analysis will reveal gaps in the knowledge, contrasts of opinions and findings, agreements and disagreements about theory and research, and indications for further research (see example in Table 8.1).

8.4 How Do You Choose the Methodological Research Framework?

Once you have formulated your questions you need to think about *how* you are going to conduct your research to provide possible answers. How are you going to do it? The methodology (e.g. experiment, observation, case study, psycholingustic methods, mixed research framework, etc.) you will select is the operating model which will provide you with the tools to conduct the study (see Table 8.2 for a description of the characteristics of the main research frameworks).

The methodological research framework you choose will depend on the purpose and the research questions of the study. Don't think about the *how* before you have established the *what* and *why*. Very often we use the one we already know as it has been used in the research papers we have read. It is important that we choose the one that can provide the best answer to our research questions.

As you review each research methodological framework to consider whether the description fits the way you envisioned your research investigation, you need to determine how the data collection and analysis will be conducted. This will help you to make very important decisions for your own study. The experimental framework will be drawing on previous studies to test or confirm hypotheses. The data collection is quantitative in nature and statistical techniques are usually used to summarize the

Table 8.2 Research frameworks

Research frameworks	*Type*	*Main Collection instruments*	*Analysis procedures*
Case study	Qualitative	Interviews Questionnaires Diaries	Content
Observation	Qualitative Quantitative	Observation schemes Tests	Content Statistical
Experimental	Quantitative	Tests Questionnaires	Statistical
Action research	Qualitative Quantitative	Tests Questionnaire	Content Statistical

information. Descriptive frameworks describe phenomena as they occur. They are used to identify and obtain information on the characteristics of a particular issue and in some cases to analyze and explain why or how something is happening. The data collected are often qualitative in nature. There is no consensus about how to actually undertake most research. Data collection procedures can supply quantitative data (numbers and statistics) or qualitative data (usually words or text). Quantitative data includes tests and surveys, and attempts to test hypotheses or statements with a view to generalizing from the specific data that you have collected. This approach typically concentrates on measuring or counting, and involves collecting and analyzing numerical data and applying statistical tests. Qualitative data use data instruments such as interviews, diaries and questionnaires to generate hypotheses from the data collection rather than testing a hypothesis. Qualitative and quantitative data are not clear-cut or mutually exclusive. More recent research frameworks make use of both quantitative and qualitative data. The difference between qualitative and quantitative research in second language acquisition is based on the overall approach to research (process- vs product-oriented) and on the emphasis and main objectives of the study (data-driven vs hypothesis-driven).

There are three possible models of integrating methodology for second language research. In the first model, a qualitative research framework contributes to the development of quantitative instruments (e.g. questionnaire construction). The second model consists of a primarily quantitative study that uses qualitative results to help interpret or explain the quantitative findings. In the third model, the two frameworks and data instruments are used equally and in parallel to cross-validate and build upon each other's results. A mixed research framework which uses both qualitative and quantitative measures can be ideal and useful to help us to increase research validity and reliability.

8.5 How Do You Choose the Data Collection and Analysis Procedures?

Data are the main component of research. Data provide a connection between a theory and the application of the theory to real world. Data make our research scientific and provide us with the empirical evidence to answer the questions raised. No data, no party!

In a quantitative and experimental research framework, data collection instruments will mainly include tests and questionnaires. In a qualitative

TASK
Read a study which has used a mixed research framework and is both qualitative and quantitative in nature.

Answer the following questions:

1. What is the main purpose of the study?
2. What is the framework used and why was it used?
3. What data collection instruments were used?

Figure 8.3 Task

approach (case study and observation framework, for instance), data collection will mainly include questionnaires, interviews, diaries and various observation techniques. You choose a particular instrument or instruments because they are considered the best way of providing empirical evidence to address the questions you have raised in the study. Whether you decide to use existing data collection instruments, to adapt them or to design completely new ones, the first attempt nearly always reveals unexpected difficulties. These may require the revision and refinement of the instrument to ensure validity and reliability. Validity in research is achieved when we have successfully measured what was originally planned. Reliability is related to whether our research is repeatable.

The adoption of a particular data collection instrument determines the type of analysis, qualitative (descriptive) or quantitative (statistical), all depending on the data available (numbers, words, etc.).

8.6 How Do You Pull Everything Together?

This is the part where the research cycle ends. You will present the main findings with the hope that you can provide answers to your original questions. Data obtained must be interpreted and discussed in relation to the literature you have reviewed at the beginning of this journey. Your discussion will include a reflection on the significance of the results and the possible multiple implications for research theory, methodology and practice. You will need to indicate limitations of the study and areas for further research which should be explored by other researchers.

When you write the conclusion of your paper/dissertation you need to remind the reader of the main thesis/objectives of the paper so they are reminded of the argument and solutions you proposed. The conclusion is where the main points, as puzzle pieces, all fit together to create a bigger picture. The reader should walk away with the bigger picture in mind! No new ideas are introduced in the conclusion. The only new idea would be suggesting a direction for future research.

You should describe and explain your research methods, and justify your decision to use them, in the main body. Your Appendices should contain blank copies of all your research instruments (questionnaires, observation sheets etc.), together with translations into English if necessary. You should provide samples of completed questionnaires, etc., and tables of the information that you have obtained. Very often these tables can be based on the research instrument itself – for example, you can replace individual responses to a questionnaire item or test scores with an average of all the responses or scores. In other cases it may be more sensible to construct new tables, for example with one row for each of your students and one column for each observed activity, questionnaire item, or whatever you wish to present. You should also include sample photocopies of students' work, if these help to illustrate your findings, as well as transcripts (and translations) of relevant interview data, etc. Raw data materials can also be presented in the appendix.

In reporting a study and its results, whether it is in the format of a paper or a dissertation, the following headings should be used:

Introduction
Background (literature review)
Motivation and purpose of the study
Design
Results
Interpretation, discussion and conclusion

The introduction should be the last part you write. The introduction is a synopsis of the various components of your study. The background section is where the researcher discusses the purpose of the study, the significance of the problem and the questions to be addressed. This section contains your literature review, in which you provide a survey of the major findings of the relevant studies, with a discussion of how they were obtained and what can be learned (critique) from them, particularly in relation to the specific research you raised at the end of the review. The main purpose of the literature review is to provide a theoretical framework for the study you want to conduct and a description of how different studies could contribute to the topic. You will then spell out the main reason for your study, the purpose and its main objectives. The research methodological framework will be presented in detail, highlighting data collection and analysis procedures. Common components are: a description of the subjects involved, the procedures used to select them, and the type and form of data collected. Results will be summarized and interpreted in the final section of your report. This part consists of a summary statement of the research results you have obtained, and then a discussion of their meaning in relation to previous literature and in the broader field of enquiry. The conclusion includes the contribution of the results to the general field of research, their methodological, theoretical and practical implications, and whether the results can lead to recommendations and suggestions for further research. Remember that in order to be successful in carrying out research you should keep in mind the following three rules:

- Select a topic that interests and fascinates you, a question you always wondered about. Keep in mind that the Latin root of 'to study' is *studio* and means 'passion'.
- Select a topic that is manageable within the time constraint. Do not try too much. Keep in mind that simplicity is a virtue, particularly in research.
- Do not give up! Frustration is the force behind much good and innovative research, and perseverance is one of the major ingredients of constructive research.

References

Allen, P., Fröhlich, M., & Spada, N. (1984). The communicative orientation of language teaching: An observation scheme. In J. Handscombe, R. Orem, & B Taylor, (Eds.), *On TESOL '83: The Question of Control* (pp. 231–252). Washington, DC: TESOL.

Allwright, D. (1988). *Observation in the Language Classroom*. London: Longman.

American Psychological Association. (2010). *Publication Manual of the American Psychological Association*. Washington, DC: American Psychological Association.

Ammar, A., & Spada, N. (2006). One size fits all?: Recasts, prompts, and L2 learning. *Studies in Second Language Acquisition*, *28*(04), 543–574. http://dx.doi.org/10.1017/S0272263106060268

Benati, A. (2001). A comparative study of the effects of processing instruction and output-based instruction on the acquisition of the Italian future tense. *Language Teaching Research*, *5*(2), 95–127.

Benati, A. (2004). The effects of processing instruction and its components on the acquisition of gender agreement in Italian. *Language Awareness*, *13*(2), 67–80. http://dx.doi.org/10.1080/09658410408667087

Benati, A. (2005). The effects of processing instruction, traditional instruction and meaning–output instruction on the acquisition of English simple past tense. *Language Teaching Research*, *9*(1), 67–93. http://dx.doi.org/10.1191/1362168805lr154oa

Benati, A. & Lee, J. (2008). *Grammar Acquisition and Processing Instruction: Secondary And Cumulative Effects*. Clevedon: Multilingual Matters.

Benati, A., & Lee, J. (2010). Exploring the effects of processing instruction on discourse-level interpretation tasks with English past tense. In A. Benati & J. Lee. *Processing Instruction and Discourse*, (pp. 178–197). London: Continuum.

Benati, A., Lee, J., & Hikima, N. (2010). Exploring the effects of processing instruction on discourse-level interpretation tasks with the Japanese passive construction. In A. Benati & J. Lee. *Processing Instruction and Discourse*, (pp. 148–177). London: Continuum.

Brown, D. (2001). *Teaching by Principles: An Interactive Approach to Language Pedagogy*. London: Longman.

Brown, J.D., & Rodgers, T. (2002). *Doing Second Language Research*. Oxford: Oxford University.

Burns, A. (2005). Action research. In E. Hinkel (Ed.), *Handbook of Research in Second Language Teaching and Learning*, (pp. 241–256). Mahwah, NJ: Lawrence Erlbaum.

Burns, A. (2010). *Doing Action Research in English Language Teaching: A Guide to Practitioners*. New York, NY: Routledge.

Canale, M. (1983). From communicative competence to communicative language pedagogy. In J. Richards, & R. Schmidt, (Eds.), *Language and Communication,* (pp. 2–27). London: Longman.

Casanave, C. (2010). Case studies. In B. Paltridge, & A. Phakti (Eds.). *Continuum Companion to Research Methods in Applied Linguistics* (pp. 66–79). London: Continuum.

Cohen, L., Manion, L., & Morrison, K. (2000). *Research Methods in Education.* London: Routledge. http://dx.doi.org/10.4324/9780203224342

Cook, T., & Campbell, D. (1979). *Quasi Experimentation: Design and Analytical Issues for Field Settings*. Chicago, IL: Rand McNally.

Creswell, J. (1994). *Research Design: Qualitative and Quantitative Approaches.* California: SAGE.

Creswell, J. (2002). *Educational Research: Planning, Conducting, and Evaluating Quantitative and Qualitative Research.* Upper Saddle River, NJ: Merrill Prentice Hall.

Creswell, J. (2003). *Research Design: Qualitative, Quantitative, and Mixed Methods Approaches* (2nd ed.). Thousands Oaks, CA: SAGE.

Creswell, J. (2005). *Educational Research: Planning, Conducting, and Evaluating Quantitative and Qualitative Research* (2nd ed.). Upper Saddle River, NJ: Merrill Prentice Hall.

Creswell, J. (2008). *Educational Research: Planning, Conducting and Evaluating Quantitative and Qualitative Research* (3rd ed.). Upper Saddle River, NJ: Pearson.

Creswell, J., & Plano Clark, L. (2007). *Designing and Conducting Mixed Methods Research.* Thousand Oaks, CA: SAGE.

De Jong, N. (2005). Can second language grammar be learned through listening? An experimental study. *Studies in Second Language Acquisition*, *27*, 205–234. http://dx.doi.org/10.1017/S0272263105050114

Dörnyei, Z. (2007). *Research Methods in Applied Linguistics.* New York: Oxford University Press.

Dörnyei, Z. (2009). The L2 motivational self system. In Z. Dörnyei, & E. Ushioda, (Eds.), *Motivation, Language Identity and the L2 Self,* (pp. 9–42). Bristol: Multilingual Matters.

Dörnyei, Z. (2010). *Questionnaires in Second Language Research: Construction, Administration, and Processing*. London: Routledge.

Dörnyei, Z., & Taguchi, T. (2010). *Questionnaires in Second Language Research. Construction, Administration, and Processing*. New York, NY: Routledge.

Duff, P. (2008). *Case Study Research in Applied Linguistics.* New York, NY: Routledge.

Ellis, R. (1997). SLA and language pedagogy: An educational perspective. *Studies in Second Language Acquisition*, *19*(01), 69–92. http://dx.doi.org/10.1017/S0272263197001058

Ellis, R. (2003). *Task-based Language Learning and Teaching*. Oxford/New York, NY: Oxford Applied Linguistics.

Fanselow, J. (1987). *Breaking Rules: Generating and Exploring Alternatives in Language Teaching*. New York, NY: Longman.

Farley, A. (2004). The relative effects of processing instruction and meaning-based output instruction. In B. VanPatten (Ed.), *Processing Instruction: Theory, Research, and Commentary*, (pp. 143–168). Mahwah, NJ: Erlbaum.

Farrell, T., & Choo, P. (2005). Conceptions of grammar teaching: A case study of teachers' beliefs and classroom practices. *TESL-EJ*, *9*, 1–13.

Felser, C., & Roberts, L. (2007). Processing wh-dependencies in a second language: A cross-modal priming study. *Second Language Research*, *23*(1), 9–36. http://dx.doi.org/10.1177/0267658307071600

Flanders, N. (1970). *Analyzing Teaching Behavior*. Reading, MA: Addison-Wesley Publications.

Flyman-Mattsson, A. (1999) Students' communicative behaviour in a foreign language classroom. *Working Papers*, *47*, 39–57.

Fotos, S., & Ellis, R. (1991). Communicating about grammar: A task-based approach. *TESOL Quarterly*, *25*(4), 605–628. http://dx.doi.org/10.2307/3587079

Frenck-Mestre, C. (2005). Eye-movement recording as a tool for studying syntactic processing in a second language: A review of methodologies and experimental findings. *Second Language Research*, *21*(2), 175–198. http://dx.doi.org/10.1191/0267658305sr257oa

Fröhlich, M., Spada, N., & Allen, P. (1985). Differences in the communicative orientation of L2 classrooms. *TESOL Quarterly*, *19*, 27–57.

Gass, S., & Mackey, A. (2000). *Stimulated Recall Methodology in Second Language Research*. New York, NY: Routledge.

Gass, S., & Mackey, A. (2005). *Second Language Research. Methodology and Design*. Mahwah, NJ: Lawrence Erlbaum Associates.

Greenwood, D., & Levin, M. (2007). *Introduction to Action Research: Social Research for Social Change*. Thousand Oaks, CA: SAGE.

Griffee, D. (2004). Research tips: Validity and history. *Journal of Developmental Education*, *28*, 1–38.

Guilloteaux, M., & Dörnyei, Z. (2008). Motivating language learners: A classroom-oriented investigation of the effects of motivational strategies on student motivation. *TESOL Quarterly*, *42*, 55–77.

Gurzynski-Weiss, L., & Révész, A. (2012). Tasks, teacher feedback, and learner modified output in naturally occurring classroom interaction. *Language Learning*, *62*(3), 851–879. http://dx.doi.org/10.1111/j.1467-9922.2012.00716.x

Hammersley, M. (1998). *Reading Ethnographic Research: A Critical Guide*. London: Longman.

Hamel, J. (1993). *Case Study Methods*. Thousand Oaks, CA: SAGE.

Hollyday, A. (2007). *Doing and Writing Qualitative Research*. London: SAGE.

Hopkins, D. (2002). *A Teacher's Guide to Classroom Research*. Maidenhead: Open University Press.

Jackson, C. (2008). Proficiency level and the interaction of lexical and morphosyntactic information during L2 sentence processing. *Language Learning*, *58*(4), 875–909. http://dx.doi.org/10.1111/j.1467-9922.2008.00481.x

Jegerski, J., & VanPatten, B. (2014). *Research Methods in Second Language Psycholinguistics*. New York, NY: Routledge.

Johnson, D. (1993). Classroom-oriented research in second language learning. In A. Omaggio-Hadley, & D. Johnson (Eds.), *Research in Language Learning* (pp. 1–23). Lincolnwood, IL: National Textbook Company.

Keating, G. (2009). Sensitivity to violations in gender agreement in native and non-native Spanish: An eye-movement investigation. *Language Learning*, *59*(3), 503–535. http://dx.doi.org/10.1111/j.1467-9922.2009.00516.x

Keating, G. (2014). Eye-tracking with text. In J. Jegerski, & B. VanPatten (Eds.), *Research Methods in Second Language Psycholinguistics*, (pp. 69–92). New York, NY: Routledge.

Larson-Hall, J. (2010). *A Guide to Doing Statistics in Second Language Research Using SPSS*. London: Routledge.

Lee, J. (2002). The incidental acquisition of Spanish future tense morphology through reading in a second language. *Studies in Second Language Acquisition*, *24*(1), 55–80. http://dx.doi.org/10.1017/S0272263102001031

Lee, J., & VanPatten, B. (2003). *Making Communicative Language Teaching Happen*. New York, NY: McGraw-Hill.

Lightbown, P., & Spada, N. (1993). Instruction and the development of questions in L2 classrooms. *Studies in Second Language Acquisition*, *15*(02), 205–224. http://dx.doi.org/10.1017/S0272263100011967

Litosseliti, L. (2009). *Research Methods in Linguistics*. London: Continuum.

Lyster, R., & Ranta, L. (1997). Corrective feedback and learner uptake: Negotiation of form in communicative classrooms. *Studies in Second Language Acquisition*, *20*, 51–81.

LoCastro, V. (1994). Teachers helping themselves: Classroom research and action research. *Language Teaching*, *18*, 4–7.

Long, M. (1984). Process and product in ESL program evaluation. *TESOL Quarterly*, *18*(3), 409–425. http://dx.doi.org/10.2307/3586712

Mackey, A., & Gass, S. (Eds.). (2012). *Research Methods in Second Language Acquisition: A Practical Guide*. Malden, MA: Wiley–Blackwell.

Mackey, A., Gass, S., Dörnyei, Z., & Czizér, K. (2012). *How to Design and Analyze Surveys in Second Language Acquisition Research*. Malden, MA: Wiley–Blackwell.

Marinis, T. (2003). Psycholinguistic techniques in second language acquisition research. *Second Language Research*, *19*(2), 144–161. http://dx.doi.org/10.1191/0267658303sr217ra

Markee, N. (1996). Making second language classroom research work. In J. Schachter, & S. Gass (Eds.). *Second Language Classroom Research: Issues and Opportunities*, (pp. 117–155). Mahwah, NJ: Lawrence Erlbaum.

Masson, M. (2011). Collecting student perceptions of feedback through interviews. PAAL 2011 Conference Proceedings. Hong Kong, China.

McKay, S. (2006). *Researching Second Language Classrooms*. Mahwah, NJ: Lawrence Erlbaum Associates.

McNiff, J., & Whitehead, J. (2006). *All You Need to Know About Action Research*. Thousand Oaks, CA: SAGE.

Mertler, G. (2006). *Action Research: Teachers as Researchers in the Classroom*. Thousand Oaks, CA: SAGE.

Morgan-Short, K., & Tanner, D. (2014). Event-Related Potentials (ERPs). In J. Jegerski, & B. VanPatten (Eds.), *Research Methods in Second Language Psycholinguistics*, (pp. 127–152). New York, NY: Routledge.

Nabei, T., & Swain, M. (2002). Learner awareness of recasts in classroom interaction: A case study of an adult EFL student's second language learning. *Language Awareness*, *11*(1), 43–63. http://dx.doi.org/10.1080/09658410208667045

Nunan, D. (1992). *Research Methods in Language Learning*. Cambridge: Cambridge Language Teaching Library.

Nunan, D. (1989). *Understanding Language Classrooms: A Guide for Instructors Initiated Action*. New York, NY: Prentice-Hall.

Nunan, D. (1990). Action research in the language classroom. In J.C. Richards, & D. Nunan (Eds.), *Second Language Teacher Education* (pp. 62–81). Cambridge: Cambridge University Press.

Nunan, D. (2005). Classroom research. In E. Hinkel (Ed.), *Handbook of Research in Second Language Teaching and Learning*, (pp. 225–240). Mahwah, NJ: Lawrence Erlbaum.

Nunan, D., & Bailey, K. (2009). *Exploring Second Language Classroom Research: A Comprehensive Guide*. Boston, MA: Heinle Cengage Learning.

Oliver, R. (1995). Negative Feedback in Child NS-NNS Conversation. *Studies in Second Language Acquisition, 17*, 459–481.

Oliver, P. (2010). *The Student's Guide to Research Ethics*. Maidenhead: Open University Press.

Omaggio-Hadley, A., & Johnson, D. (Eds.). (1993). *Research in Language Learning*. Lincolnwood, IL: National Textbook Company.

Otha, A. (1995). Applying sociocultural theory to analysis of learner discourse: Collaborative interaction in the zone of proximal development. *Issues in Applied Linguistics*, *6*(2), 93–121.

Paltridge, B., & Phakti, A. (Eds.). (2010). *Continuum Companion to Research Methods in Applied Linguistics*. London: Continuum.

Pine, G. (2009). *Teacher Action Research*. Thousand Oaks, CA: SAGE.

Plano Clark, L., & Creswell, J. (2008). *The Mixed Methods Reader*. Thousand Oaks, CA: SAGE.

Rasinger, S. (2013). *Quantitative Research in Linguistics*. London: Bloomsbury.

Richards, K., Ross, S., & Seedhouse, P. (2012). *Research Methods for Applied Language Studies*. New York, NY: Routledge.

Roberts, L. (2012). Psycholinguistic techniques and resources in second language acquisition research. *Second Language Research*, *28*(1), 113–127. http://dx.doi.org/10.1177/0267658311418416

Roberts, L., & Lizska, S.A. (2013). Processing tense/aspect-agreement violations on-line in the second language: A self-paced reading study with French and German L2 learners of English. *Second Language Research*, *29*(4), 413–439. http://dx.doi.org/10.1177/0267658313503171

Roberts, L., Gullberg, M., & Indefrey, P. (2008). Online pronoun resolution in L2 discourse: L1 influence and general learner effects. *Studies in Second Language Acquisition*, *30*(03), 333–357. http://dx.doi.org/10.1017/S0272263108080480

Sampson, R. (2012). The language-learning self, self-enhancement activities, and self perceptual change. *Language Teaching Research*, *16*(3), 317–335. http://dx.doi.org/10.1177/1362168812436898

Sato, M. (2013). Beliefs about peer interaction and peer corrective feedback: Efficacy of classroom intervention. *Modern Language Journal*, *97*(3), 611–633. http://dx.doi.org/10.1111/j.1540-4781.2013.12035.x

Schmidt, R. (1995). Consciousness and foreign language learning: A tutorial on the role of attention and awareness in learning. In R. Schmidt (Ed.), *Attention and Awareness in Foreign Language Learning*, (pp. 1–64). Honolulu: University of Hawai'i.

Schmidt, R., & Frota, S. (1986). Developing basic conversational ability in a second language. A case study of an adult learner of Portuguese. In R. Day (ed.), *Talking to Learn: Conversation in Second Language Acquisition*, (pp. 237–326). Rowley, MA: Newbury House.

Schwandt, T. (2007). *The SAGE Dictionary of Qualitative Inquiry*. Thousand Oaks, CA: SAGE.

Scott, K., Kolano, Q., & Wang C. (2010). Perceptions of gender differences in high school students' motivation to learn Spanish. *Foreign Language Annals*, *43*(2), 703–721.

Seliger, H., & Shohamy, E. (1989). *Second Language Research Methods*. Oxford: Oxford University Press.

Shadish, W., Cook, T., & Campbell, D. (2002). *Experimental and Quasi-Experimental Designs for Generalized Causal Inference*. Boston, MA: Houghton Mifflin.

Shadish, W., & Luellen, J. (2006). Quasi-experimental design. In J.L. Green, G. Camilli, & P.B. Elmore (Eds.), *Handbook of Complementary Methods in Education Research*, (pp. 539–550). Mahwah, NJ: Erlbaum.

Spada, N. (1986). The interaction between type of contact and type of instruction: Some effects on the L2 proficiency of adult learners. *Studies in Second Language Acquisition*, *8*(02), 181–199. http://dx.doi.org/10.1017/S0272263100006070

Spada, N. (1987). Relationships between instructional differences and learning outcomes: A process–product study of communicative language teaching. *Applied Linguistics*, *8*(2), 137–161. http://dx.doi.org/10.1093/applin/8.2.137

Spada, N. (1990). Observing classroom behaviours and learning outcomes in different second language programs. In J.C. Richards & D. Nunan (Eds.), *Second Language Teacher Education*, (pp. 293–310). Cambridge: Cambridge University Press.

Spada, N., & Lyster, R. (1997). Macroscopic and microscopic views of L2 classrooms. *TESOL Quarterly*, *31*(4), 787–792. http://dx.doi.org/10.2307/3587763

Steinhauer, K., White, E., & Drury, J. (2009). Temporal dynamics of late second language acquisition: Evidence from event-related brain potentials. *Second Language Research*, *25*(1), 13–41. http://dx.doi.org/10.1177/0267658308098995

Stringer, E. (2007). *Action Research*. Thousand Oaks, CA: SAGE.

Toth, P. (2006). Processing instruction and a role for output in second language acquisition. *Language Learning*, *56*(2), 319–385. http://dx.doi.org/10.1111/j.0023-8333.2006.00349.x

Ullmann, R., & Geva, E. (1982). *The Target Language Observation Scheme (TALOS). New York Board of Education, Core French Evaluation Project*. Toronto: Ontario Institute for Studies in Education.

VanPatten, B., & Benati, A. (2010). *Second Language Acquisition: Key Terms*. London: Continuum.

VanPatten, B., Borst, S., Collopy, E., Qualin, A., & Price, J. (2013). Explicit information, grammatical sensitivity, and the first-noun strategy: A cross-linguistic study in processing instruction. *Modern Language Journal*, *97*(2), 506–527. http://dx.doi.org/10.1111/j.1540-4781.2013.12007.x

Wajnryb, R. (1993). *Classroom Observation Tasks: A Resource Book for Language Teachers and Trainers*. Cambridge: Cambridge University Press.

Wei, L., & Moyer, M. (Eds.). (2008). *The Blackwell Guide to Research Methods in Bilingualism and Multilingualism*. Oxford: Blackwell.

Wesche, M., & Paribakht, S. (2000). Reading-based exercises in second language vocabulary learning: An introspective study. *Modern Language Journal*, *84*(2), 196–213. http://dx.doi.org/10.1111/0026-7902.00062

Index

www.ingramcontent.com/pod-product-compliance
Lightning Source LLC
LaVergne TN
LVHW010444080826
844660LV00026B/1217